HOW TO FIX THE WORLD (IN 3 EASY STEPS)

How to
Fix the World

(in 3 Easy Steps)

Joshua W. Hunking

HOUNDSTOOTH
PRESS

HOW TO FIX THE WORLD (IN 3 EASY STEPS)

FIRST EDITION

ISBN   978-1-5445-4506-6   *Hardcover*

        978-1-5445-4505-9   *Paperback*

        978-1-5445-4504-2   *Ebook*

I dedicate this book to all those people who helped me over the course of my life. Without you I could never be me; I hope that my effort spent in this endeavor has the ability to help someone else be better than they otherwise would. Oh yeah...and to my darling wife, Heatherlee.

Contents

Introduction

TL;DR: If we incentivize the generation of better ideas by creating a system to control the economic value of the idea thereby generated, we can justify the investment into the generation of the better idea and thus create the incentive to generate the better idea in the first place.

THIS BOOK INTENDS TO HELP EXPLAIN TO YOU THE BEST known method by which we can solve problems that need an idea as the solution. I will do my best to take complex ideas framed in the form of processes and make them as clear as I possibly can to any reader who is trying to understand this subject. My main goal is to persuade you that your world will get better if you use better tools to generate ideas to make it better.

I am a lawyer from the Willamette Valley in Oregon. Specifically, I am a trial lawyer who understands the rules surrounding the driving of vehicles in Oregon better than almost anyone else in the world. I am also a human, and more specifically a human with a brain that operates in a particular way. If you asked me to generate abstract art you would be disappointed with the results. But if you asked me to generate a process by which you can effectuate an outcome, you would be pleasantly surprised with the result you got. Because my brain happens to understand processes better than most other people I have met, I tend to use processes as a way to understand the world.

By way of anecdote, in law school I vividly remember having discussions in constitutional law class about what happens when one constitutional principle comes into conflict with another constitutional principle. The other students seemed to intrinsically understand something that I, to this day, do not understand. From my perspective, arguments about which right is superior and why just don't seem to resonate—or frankly, even be a conversation worth having. Don't worry, I still got a B+ (I think) in constitutional law because I can understand and apply the rules, but I did substantially better compared to my peers in Civil Procedure, Property Law, and Intellectual Property Law because those subjects are really just about the rules of process. They are black and white and flow chronologically to effectuate an outcome.

In my job, I am regularly standing next to a person who is accused of drunk driving and arguing to the Judge whether they should go to jail for three days, seven days, thirty days, or not at all. What I know to be true through experience over time is that it is irrelevant how many days you put a person in jail for drinking and driving if your goal is to get them to not do it again. Which then caused me to wonder why I can continue to tell people the same thing over the course of several years and still always achieve the same result—that no one seems to understand that the actions we are taking in the criminal justice system, specifically relating to drunk driving (but also to other areas), do nothing to impact the likelihood that someone will not drink and drive in the future. Facing this problem and feeling like I am beating my head into a wall trying to get people to understand the obvious truth led me down a path to attempt to understand why these problems seem very solvable to me, but we collectively fail to solve these problems or even make progress on them in any reasonable period of time. It clicked in my head about two years ago, and I have been refining ever since. With this book I hope to explain to everyone what I now know to be provably and inexorably true.

If you stick around and really grapple with these concepts you will see the passive benefit to your life and the life of your progeny that will necessarily occur as a result of your acceptance of (and nonresistance to) the very basic principles I am about to get into.

The ultimate goal is to show you that by leveraging intellectual property law as the primary tool to generate better ideas, we can create better ideas. I will explain the underlying systems that create the interactions that force the result. By which I mean that whether you like it or not, rules work collectively to create systems, those systems result in a response from people, those responses create an outcome. I intend to show you how those rules create our current systems, which will show you why we have the results we have. In knowing that, you will be able to see, as I do, why some minor changes to the rules will result in substantially better outcomes much faster than we would otherwise achieve those outcomes. I will discuss the basic purpose, design, and effect of property law (at least in the American system), specifically what intellectual property law is and why it exists and what effect it has. Once all of this is understood, you'll see why the invariable and obvious truth is that in order to make a better world, we need to apply intellectual property law rules to every type of problem that we want to solve.

Of course, I am not able to see all potential unintended consequences because this hasn't been studied yet. But anecdotally, I believe it will work because (1) when I turn on the radio I hear amazing songs for free, (2) when I go to the store I see very useful kitchen gadgets that I would never have thought of at bargain basement prices, and (3) I compare the improvements in medicine to the improvements in the justice system over the last 150 years. The rules of intellectual property are already working, and they are helping us solve problems faster than any other system known to humans.

The purpose of this book is to reorient the way you see problem-solving. If we need a better idea in order to solve a problem, how can we generate that better idea? Let me show you.

CHAPTER 1

How We Currently Solve Public Policy Problems (and Why It Is Potentially Less Effective than Other Ways to Solve Public Policy Problems. Stated Another Way, "What Is the Problem We Are Attempting to Evaluate and Solve?")

THE PROBLEM WITH OUR CURRENT SYSTEM OF SOLVING public policy problems is that it fails to operate effectively and efficiently in getting the job done. I can give a thousand examples of this: (1) the DMV takes an unreasonably long period of time to get simple tasks completed, (2) the military wastes a lot of money on a lot of silly things that don't make our world safer, (3) we haven't decreased the likelihood that a drunk driver is going to kill someone, (4) we haven't solved gun violence, (5) in Oregon we have outlawed the possession of magazines that hold over ten rounds with no idea whether that will impact gun violence, (6) we allow homeless people to live on the streets regardless of the cost to the taxpayer or harm to the person or businesses, (7) drugs are still easily accessible to anyone who tries to find them and addicts continue to find them, (8) etc. I could go on and on and on, but I doubt anyone disagrees that our current model of public policy generation is not very good at getting things done efficiently and effectively.

Many problems require an idea as a solution—as opposed to a physical object or product—to solve it. One area that needs ideas as a solution more than most is the arena of public policy. Today, ideas are discussed and protected within the realm of intellectual property law. I am convinced that the intellectual property law system is the better avenue through which we should pursue solutions to public policy problems.

You may be wondering why I would say that intellectual property law will help us solve any problem that needs an idea as a solution. You may be thinking to yourself, what problem doesn't need an idea to solve it? I can give you an example: I want my wife to feel loved even though I know that I will be gone by the time she wakes up. In order to effectuate that goal I grab a piece of paper (which I did not manufacture myself, nor design myself) and a ballpoint pen (which I did not manufacture myself, nor design myself) and I write in the English language (which I did not create myself, nor design myself) the words "I love you" and leave the paper in a conspicuous place where I know she will find it when she wakes up. In order to solve the problem of how to ensure that my wife feels loved even though I won't be there when she wakes up, I simply use things created by others to solve the problem. I don't need an idea to create a language, nor a written language, nor a method by which I can express and store that written language. Those problems have already been solved, and in my sense of the phrase, you simply would not need an idea to solve that problem. Someone else has already solved that problem for me and made it very easy to solve.

The problems I am discussing are those where we really don't have known and agreed ideas available to solve problems. For example, how do you stop a shoplifter from shoplifting? How do you get a drunk driver to stop drinking and driving? What punishment can you impose on a trespasser to get the trespasser to stop trespassing? How can you convince a homeless person to move indoors? How do you restore faith in police officers among people who have been oppressed by police for a long time? How do you stop Russia from moving troops into territory that Ukraine believes it owns? How do you identify a future school shooter? How do you keep kids safe from both their defective parents and the foster care system they would otherwise enter? Can you rehabilitate the parents? Can you improve the foster care system? Would another system entirely be a better solution for keeping kids safe and healthy? How do you reduce the global carbon footprint? This list goes on forever, but I believe I have been clear that solving problems that need an idea as a solution simply means solving those problems we haven't solved yet.

With regard to making public policy in the United States, I believe the American founding fathers firmly believed that the best way to accomplish that was raucous public debate. They debated in legislative chambers, they wrote articles in the paper, and they advocated for their beliefs to the greatest of their abilities. As far as I can tell this was a reasonably effective way to generate public policy.

However, does anyone in the modern world look to the halls of Congress for substantive debate about the merits of varying public policies? I don't know of anyone who does. From my perspective our modern Congress gets its detailed policy work done by staffers who work well outside the view of the public. Most public discourse currently seems to not actually engage a differing opinion or policy choice at all, but rather to try and stir up enough public and monetary support for the position they already believe in to have their position win the day.[1]

Further, back in 1791, several unique factors necessarily limited the scope of congressional debate: the total population in the United States was just under four million people and only White men over twenty-one who owned land were eligible to vote. Thus, a raucous public debate among all available voters was a realistic way to generate good public policy ideas at the time. Today, though, this system is no longer able to work well due to population alone.

Robert Dahl recognized this problem long ago, and I first learned of it in his book *On Democracy*. There, he argues consistently and (in my opinion) persuasively that the structure of a democracy must necessarily change based on the size of it due to the natural consequences of the inherent limitations of humans within a four-dimensional world. I explain this to my employees (and anyone who will listen) as a simple logic problem. How long would it take for you to have a five-minute conversation with everyone on the planet? The answer in 2023 is pretty simple because you will die long before you are able to speak to everyone for even five minutes. Hundreds of humans are born every minute. You are slipping further from your goal every single time you speak to a person for five minutes. Even among eligible voters in the United States it would be an impossible task. According to the internet, a human is born every eight seconds in the United States. You

---

[1] It should be noted that no portion of the ideas in this book should be construed to subvert the democratic policy-making system. That system is effective (ish) at allowing us to live in a world that has rules that most accurately reflect the will of the people subjected to those rules. The purpose of this book is simply to explain to people (meaning you, the human reading this) that if you allow ownership of an idea that makes a public policy system better (e.g., fixing homelessness) then using the systems we already have in place you can create those ideas more effectively and efficiently so that our democratically elected leaders have the ability to use those solutions for our benefit. We don't want to supplant the democratic system entirely, for reasons not explored further in this book.

can never know the interests of every eligible voter on a single topic within your lifetime; quite simply, there are too many of us for that to be even remotely possible, which creates problems for the problem-solving model of raucous public debate.

One result of those early public debates that has proven hugely successful: Article I, Section 8, Clause 8 of the United States Constitution states in pertinent part, "To promote the progress of science and useful arts, by securing for limited times to authors and inventors the exclusive right to their respective writings and discoveries." That clause is pretty simple in its mandate; it tells the Congress that they have the power to promote the progress of science and useful arts by giving artists and inventors time-limited licenses to their ideas. Congress, in fact, does this by creating, on a federal level, the intellectual property laws of the United States. I think of these intellectual property laws as the system by which we create better ideas.

Intellectual Property Law System vs. Current System of Public Policy Development

Recently, we all had the perfect opportunity to witness public policy creation in action. Between 2019 and 2022, the United States dealt with both the arrival in the US of COVID-19 (I mean the virus itself, which I consider to be an invisible thing that didn't previously exist) and George Floyd's death and the resultant public outrage. These events required significant public policy actions, but were handled very differently, with differing degrees of success.

Managing the government's response to COVID-19 had its public policy components, but there was also the science component of developing a vaccine. In raw terms of the virus itself, because of systems designed to create better ideas (i.e., our intellectual property laws) scientists were able to quickly develop treatments and vaccines to solve what was perceived as a problem (contracting the virus and potentially dying therefrom). All of this is made possible because companies put into place organizations of human effort designed for exactly this purpose—to generate new ideas.

The company I will use as a reference point is Pfizer. Pfizer was apparently founded in 1849 and since then it has built and built to become what it was in 2019. Its business model is made possible because of intellectual property law. It hires smart people and tasks them with generating new ideas to solve problems within a particular area (biotechnology and pharmaceuticals). They are able to justify the paychecks of the scientists by the hope that the scientists will create good ideas that are novel and unobvious (as you will see, this means patentable), which they then gain a legal right to control and can sell as an idea itself, or in the alternative they can build the products themselves and sell the final product to humans who need the final product (or a government that wants a COVID-19 vaccine).

The end result for my life, from my limited viewpoint, is that I get a treatment and a vaccine for COVID-19 that sufficiently convinces my government that it will be safe for me to roam the world, such that I am able to roam the world and get back to solving the problems I am tasked with solving for this society. None of this could have happened without deliberate and directed human effort and intellect and energy applied toward solving the problem. These systems (Pfizer) were able to spring into action quickly because the infrastructure was already in place. The only difference for them was that instead of trying to fix cancer or AIDS or whatever, they were directed toward fixing the COVID-19 issue. And all that human effort and energy cost me was the low, low price of a few tax dollars.

Simultaneously, the American public policy system sprang into action and did the best it could to solve the problem of outrage after the death of George Floyd. The end result thus far? A few humans got imprisoned, some police departments stopped using chokeholds, and a few other jurisdictions tried to change some policies that were perceived to be relics of a racist system or are otherwise harmful to Black people. Because our system of public policy making relies so heavily on elected leaders, they really aren't equipped to solve the problems they are supposed to solve.

Ask yourself which problem seems more insurmountable in raw terms: (a) identifying and vaccinating against a potentially deadly virus or (b) resolving a feeling/belief that if you are a certain color, your government will treat you unfairly (or might even kill you). Then ask yourself, which problem seems more solved?

For me, responding to COVID-19 seemed a much more difficult problem and the solution more challenging to identify. For thousands of years of human history, we didn't even know viruses existed. Yet, within twenty-four months, today's scientists developed multiple vaccines to attack and limit COVID-19's severity. In contrast, every day when I look at my news feed I see another example of a potential source of outrage. On the day that I wrote this paragraph, for example, I used Reddit and happened across a video of a police officer in Tennessee who attempted to take a Black woman into custody. The woman did not want to go into custody and, in the video, claimed to have done nothing wrong (I can't render an opinion on the truth or veracity of that without the background information, which was not included in the video). As a result, the police officer escalated the situation and tased the woman while she tried to get in her car and drive away, the woman pulled a gun and shot the officer in the side, he shot her back, and she died shortly after crashing her car while attempting to drive away. Regardless of if/what the woman did wrong, did we really need to have a conflict between a police officer and a citizen that resulted in gun-shots, an injured officer, a dead citizen, and a crashed car? Is there not a better way to attempt to resolve conflict within the criminal sphere? I submit to you that there clearly is, and with just a little intellectual effort and human energy, we can empirically gather and analyze information sufficient to let us at least begin diagnosing and resolving the problem.

Clearly, the virus problem seems more solved. I believe that is because of the speed and quality of ideas generated by the machinations of intellectual property law as opposed to those resulting from raucous public debate. These above examples show how and why we are able to produce better ideas more quickly when we employ different tools—specifically those tools of intellectual property—to effectuate that goal. As we saw with COVID-19, the quick development of the vaccine was only possible because intellectual property law had (1) preserved scientific information that had been gained over the last hundred years, (2) incentivized further development of that knowledge, and (3) preserved and pro-tected the knowledge and products that were currently being developed. Without a system like IP, all that knowledge would probably have been lost.

The Intellectual Property System Is the Best Way We Are Currently Aware of to Effectively Generate, Sort, Store, Organize, and Convey Human Knowledge

WHY IS IT THAT IP LAW SYSTEMS ARE BETTER THAN JUST using human minds to hold all the information necessary to solve a problem? Because the limitations in the human form make it a less efficient system by which we hold information than the systems employed under IP law.

The human form truly is terribly inefficient at gaining and storing knowledge. Frankly, this is something we already know to be true intrinsically. We must realize the basic fact that humans die. Further, that there is an extremely high like-lihood that you will die, that I will die, and that everyone who is alive today will eventually die. Next, we must acknowledge that more humans are being born today and presumably will be for the foreseeable future. Those humans will take decades to learn and grow and develop such that they have knowledge that you and I already have. I know how to count, and to speak, and to tie my shoes. A human that is currently two months old has yet to learn those things. Thus, human existence is a perpetually inefficient cycle of old humans dying and taking their knowledge with them when they go, which new humans must then painstakingly learn over the course of their lives. The system itself is terribly inefficient by design. What we commonly call wisdom is, in my limited experience, simply the cumulative value of synthesized knowledge gained over the course of years or decades of gaining knowledge. That thing we call wisdom is constantly lost due to the death of the human that has the wisdom, and is being relearned by a new human grappling to understand a thing that was once clearly known by another.

Our Natural Limitations Make Us Inefficient for Storing Knowledge Long-Term

If I was to design existence I wouldn't house it in a human body. There are inefficiencies in the way we exist that are inherent in our nature. For example, I can imagine a beautiful picture, or have an idea for an invention expressed in my mind in schematic drawings. In order to get that idea from my head to another person's head it takes a lot of time and effort. I can express the feeling of happiness with a simple smile and quickly communicate to another human (even one who doesn't speak my language) the emotion that the smile conveys, but I cannot imagine an opera and then convey it to another human in a way that they would understand without a substantially larger amount of effort. It is OK that we are limited; I can't personally change it even if I wanted to, and further, I am not sure I would change it if given the chance. But, the limitations do exist, and if left unacknowledged, then we fail to recognize the reality of the world within which we exist.

Another limitation that exists for us as humans is the limited amount of time that we will exist. In order for human knowledge to be generated a human must exist to generate it. In order for that knowledge to continue to exist beyond the life of the knowledge generator, the human must either write it down, record it somewhere, or get it into the head of another human that then keeps that knowledge. The system itself is an inefficient way to gain knowledge over time. There are things that some human absolutely knew to be correct over a hundred years ago that I am just learning to be true today. The same lessons are learned, then lost (by the death of the human who knew it), then learned again by another. The system is just not an efficient way to gather and retain knowledge. I know that it is hard to hear, but to the best of my knowledge, no one has ever been able to live forever. I guess it is technically true that those of us who currently exist may continue to exist for eternity, but it is extremely unlikely and contrary to all available evidence (that clearly humans die). For example, everyone born in the year 1500 died a long, long time ago—not just some of them—all of them, without exception.

As yet another limitation on the world within which we exist is our ability to understand different facets of existence to varying degrees. I understand that music exists. I understand that music is generally made by humans for humans. I understand that I enjoy said music. I do not, however, know how to read music or write a song. Not to mention that Taylor Swift and Kanye West likely understand how to create a song to a greater level of detail than I could likely ever understand. This is OK as well. We are human; we have limitations, and our brains function differently and will grasp and retain different types of knowledge more or less quickly than others and more or less thoroughly than others, but that's OK. Those variations allow us to accomplish a lot more together than we ever could individually.

We are also limited by our human faculties. I don't know about you, but I can only see within the visible range of the light spectrum. I can use equipment to expand the scope of what I can perceive in terms of electromagnetic energy, but currently I can't see in ultraviolet. There are things my dog can hear, but that I cannot. There are things that my dog can smell, but that I cannot. These limitations on our ability to perceive and understand the world around us are necessary parts of our humanity. It doesn't mean that things are unhearable or unsmellable or that the knowledge cannot be generated; it just means that we within our human bodies lack that capacity.

Similarly, humans have individual variations such that our capacities differ (within a range) from each other. For example, I was having lunch with a friend and the subject of ketchup came up in the context of preservatives used to keep the ketchup from spoiling. Regardless of the original purpose of the conversation, my brain couldn't help but come back to the conclusions of this book: if I was alone on this planet would I have ever invented ketchup? The answer is a resounding no, it simply would never have occurred to me to try and make a sauce. Further, I would not have the testing capacity or patience or freedom to simply try different things until I found a combination that resulted in a decent-tasting product that didn't immediately spoil. As I have said before, maybe I am a dunce, but I am virtually certain that alone on this planet by myself I wouldn't even invent a chair, I would just learn to sit on things nearby.

All of the limitations on our existence that impose themselves by virtue of the reality within which we exist are not inherently good or bad things. They just are. I enjoyed having conversations with my grandfather about the things he knew to be true. I hope that he enjoyed having those conversations with me. Those conversations are an inefficient way to gather, store, and evaluate knowledge, but they were also very human experiences that made my life better and hopefully my grandfather's life as well. So again, just to be crystal clear, limitations that exist by virtue of the world we live in aren't bad or good, they just are. The only thing to take away from this is to simply understand that those limitations are there, they impact us, and they create certain macro effects that we likely are unable to change.

The Intellectual Property System Currently Offers the Best Way to Protect and Preserve Humanity's Ideas

The intellectual property system transfers and preserves information better than any other system. In order to get a copyright you must give a copy of the work to the Library of Congress (more specifically the US Copyright Office), the library gets to keep that copy forever, and anyone who wants a copy is able to get one. In order to get a patent you must frame the patent in terms of teaching someone else how to do the thing (or make the thing) you want to patent. These systems are simply more precise, more thorough, and less subjected to the telephone game than would be passing down knowledge orally because the storage system for the ideas are precise, not subject to decay over time and not limited in the way that our human bodies are limited.

Applying intellectual property laws to public policy problems is only one example of how we can organize human effort and intellect in the most effective and efficient way. It is important to understand that just because this is one way to solve the problem, it is not the only system by which we could potentially organize ourselves. My standard analogy is that I am sitting here watching my criminal justice system try to screw together a fence using a rock, and I am holding a screwdriver begging that we use it. I am not saying that a screwdriver is the best tool, but the beauty of ideas applied to developing better public policy systems is that it can be used to improve itself. Like a robot that can design and build a better robot. Just because I have a screwdriver doesn't mean that someone way smarter than me (possibly in hundreds or thousands of years) can't develop a power drill to further improve the method by which we create these systems. And after that, someone else can create something better than a power drill that I can't even conceptualize currently due to the limits on my capacity as a human. There was certainly a day three thousand years ago when a human woke up in the morning as the most knowledgeable person on the planet and that person likely never even dreamed of the basic outline of the concept of a smartphone. Yet, here we are today and smartphones are ubiquitous. How can we not see that we are just as limited as that person once was and that in three thousand years someone will look back at us and be shocked at how little the smartest person on the planet knew compared to their fifth graders?

Many people will argue that the intellectual property legal system is flawed because, for example, it allows sick people to die since no one is allowed to make a cheaper life-saving drug. However, my response is that by using intellectual property laws and making them applicable to public policy systems, we can incentivize the creation of better systems to help mitigate the effect of this problem. If the trade-off for teaching people how to do something (i.e., making a patent that records for the public how to generate the novel and unobvious thing) is to allow for a time-limited license to control that idea, which then justifies the investment into the generation of the idea in the first place, then certainly we can find a way to limit or mitigate the most harmful effects of that. How can we most effectively and efficiently determine how to do that? Well... we could justify the investment into the generation of the solution by creating a time-limited license to control over that solution such that we can direct human effort and intellect within a capitalist system toward the generation of the solution. Stated another way, let's use the intellectual property system that we know creates the result of the generation of better ideas to generate better ideas.

If we have a system (frankly, any system) by which a human can control an idea, the incentive to create the idea remains the same, and we will in fact help all of humanity create better ideas. As long as we understand and use that basic principle the world will get better, and the really, really cool part is that it will get better at getting better even faster. I have seen plenty of memes about exactly this issue. Look at how fast technology improved over the 1900s from the invention of the airplane to landing on the moon. And today, we can accelerate even further even faster by building on the knowledge generated by humans who have long since died.

Preserving Knowledge Allows Ideas to Naturally Build upon Each Other

Conceptually I find it useful to discuss how ideas build upon each other over time using the evolution of a table as an example. At its core, a table is nothing more than a tree against which human effort and intellect has been applied. Although I don't actually know the evolution of a table (I am not sure anyone really does), I imagine it happened as follows:

Some human made the determination that they wanted to set stuff down but also to keep it off the ground. I imagine that initially a table was just a large fallen tree laying in its natural state or a flat rock that happened to be nearby. After this human made the determination that setting stuff down and off the ground was a good idea, other humans likely agreed due to its utility. Understandably they would begin to run into problems and solve them over time one by one. Initially I can imagine that a nonflat surface was less useful than a flat surface, so some human applied effort to make the holding surface flat. Additionally, I imagine that humans would have recognized that splinters were a problem and endeavored to find a way to keep the generally flat surface generally free from splinters.

In conjunction with the development of a chair, it would be recognized that a log would be less than ideal for sitting at, because the shape of a human in a chair necessitates the need to place human legs in the space under the flat surface used for holding things. I would bet that at some point someone carved a log into the general shape of a table so that humans could sit at it and place their legs under it. It would not have taken long for humans to realize that if they took other smaller parts of trees and placed them at ninety-degree angles that they could prop up the table section and allow human legs to fit under the table in a seated position.

It is notable that tables are generally designed for an average height human. I imagine this bothers the very short and very tall among us because the table itself likely does not suit their needs. That said, someone somewhere through history must have adjusted the height of a table, and slowly over time a generally accepted height for a table emerged. Japan is a great example of how this evolution may not have been uniform throughout the entire planet, but because different ideas of how a table should work in Japan emerged, they reached a different result regarding what the height of a table should be.

At some point some human began innovating the table and the process by which a table is made by learning to sand down and smooth out to a fine degree the edges and surfaces of the table. Then someone invented chemicals that could seal a table surface such that the wood would remain intact longer. Then someone invented ways to use those chemicals to make the surface of the table look more beautiful.

At some point, someone began making tables out of different materials to include metal and glass. Then, someone came up with a new type of wood made out of shavings of larger pieces of wood with chemicals applied to the shavings such that they would be bound together effectively. Then someone decided to use that type of material to make a table that can be smaller when shipped, thereby making it more efficient to ship and then assemble on your own at home.

At the end of this long compilation of ideas layered on top of each other throughout hundreds of years, we are able to enjoy the fruits of all that effort and intellect without individually investing in it. For example, as I write this, I have my feet up on a desk made of adhered wood particles that were assembled by me personally into the shape of a work desk. The exterior of the desk is some material that I would never have invented, but it looks nice, and it is functional. I have had this desk for almost ten years, and I will likely have it for another ten years. I like this desk. I bought this desk because, when I was making my purchasing decisions, I was looking at available options, and this desk suited my needs and was the cheapest available version of an object that suited my needs that was available for purchase. Thus, I purchased the desk, had it shipped to me, and assembled it myself in my office. The ideas that went into the creation of this desk far exceed the capacity that exists within me individually. Stated simply, if I started right now trying to build this desk it would take me so much time to complete it that I would be unable to use my limited time for other purposes (like writing this book, or practicing law).

Better Ideas Make the World Better

If anyone is questioning the rightness of the statement "better ideas make the world better" then let me dissuade you of any concern over whether this statement may be incorrect. A cool thing that has happened over the course of the last decade or so is that the internet has made information sharing much easier. The ease comes from several things: (1) the ability to share a video (a picture is worth a thousand words), (2) the searchability of information makes finding what you are looking for pretty easy, and (3) the technology needed to record and access and upload and download information has become extremely ubiquitous. One very cool thing that has popped up as a result of this is called a "life hack." A life hack is quite simply a better way to accomplish a task using relatively simple means. All these life hacks consist of just better ideas for solving a problem. It isn't as if the nature of solving a problem has changed, but rather the knowledge to solve the problem better or easier that is shared in such a way that it makes the receiver's approach to solving the problem a better approach. Every person that exists doesn't have to try and reinvent the wheel.

A quick Google search yielded a great immediate example of how and why a life hack makes life better. The hack simply states: "Tie a piece of bright-colored fabric to your luggage. Saves a lot of time to check if it's your bag or not." followed by a picture of a gray piece of luggage with a pink piece of fabric tied to the top. The value here is obvious: someone encountered a problem (how do I find my luggage on an airport conveyor belt when other luggage looks similar and I am not sure if this particular bag is mine?) and found a solution to that problem that they believed to be a better solution. It was simple and easy, and the receiver of the information may not have even predicted that finding their luggage would be a problem. The coolest part about this whole system is that if you disagree and don't like the idea then you just don't use it. If a better life hack comes along then that one (in theory) will rise to the top as the solution for solving the problem of spending extra time trying to find your bag at the airport when you can easily save that time, energy, and effort. As you can see, better ideas make the world better.

Understand Property Law (and Capitalism as a Function of Property Law)

CHAPTER 3

Property Laws Produce a System of Human Organization Designed to Move Property to Its Highest and Best Use

ONE OF THE BEST CLASSES I EVER TOOK IN LAW SCHOOL was property law taught by a wonderful professor named Vincent Chiappetta. He appeared to intrinsically understand what most professors didn't realize: to know how to apply a rule (meaning a law) you must understand why the rule exists and what its purpose is. Learning an area of the law by simply reading and memorizing the law is an asinine way of actually understanding how to apply the law. A much better approach (the approach used by Professor Chiappetta) is to understand why the rules are the way they are and then learn what the actual rules are. The underlying purpose of what the rules are trying to accomplish is vastly more valuable than knowing what the exact details of the rules are.

This concept is basic, but often overlooked. It is likely a result of deficiencies inherent in human language. It is unfortunate, but as things that exist within a human body, we are limited in our capacity to understand the world around us. I have senses that can perceive the world around me, but without the assistance of technology, I will never be able to see ultraviolet light simply because my eyes are not designed to see light in that spectrum. It does not change whether the ultra-violet light exists or whether it has an impact on the world around me; what remains is the simple truth that things can exist and impact my world, and I may be completely unable to perceive them.

As a part of the same problem, our ability to communicate with each other comes in a form that has limitations. I personally communicate and think in the English language. I once heard a rumor that in some native languages there are multiple words for snow such that in those languages you can discuss snow with much greater nuance than you ever could in the English language. This problem is embedded within our system of laws because, as you may be aware, we write our laws down in English as the method by which we make those laws known to the public before we attempt to enforce those rules against the public. This inherent limitation on language creates an inexorable result that you cannot simply take the words as the restatement of the law and be done with it. A quick example: in Oregon, the legislature passed a rule (law) that if you used a gun in a residential burglary that you would be subjected to a mandatory minimum term of incarceration of several years. It makes sense, doesn't it? If someone is willing to use a gun in a residential burglary they are creating an inherently dangerous situation that probably does deserve a stiff penalty, right? John, unaware of the enhancement, uses a functioning shotgun (without ammunition) to prop open the gate surrounding an expensive house as he proceeds to approach the house, enter, and complete a residential burglary. Obviously, what the legislature meant in drafting the law was any "use" of a gun, right? Even if the gun was not used as a gun, but instead as a doorstop, right? Obviously there is a different harm that exists if John carried that same shotgun with him into the home as a source of intimidation against a resident during a residential burglary. The words, as written, precisely capture a concept, but that concept does not apply equally in all circumstances, which creates a fundamentally unfair result in the real world.

Language is flexible by design, written language even more so because it lacks intonation and gesture and other nonverbal cues. It is within this context where we must find a way to read and understand the rules and apply them. Which, as above, is why it is substantially more important to understand why the rule exists as opposed to what the rule actually says. If you understand why the rule exists you can much more easily read the rule and apply the correct interpretation of that rule.

The Goals and Benefits of Property Law

The background information you will need conceptually will seem pretty basic (I think), but it is necessary to understand the building blocks in order to understand the final concept. Think of it like this: in order to read this paragraph you must first understand the English language, then you must learn how to read, then you can read this paragraph. Without the building blocks it doesn't matter what information is contained in this paragraph, you won't understand it. Let's get to the building blocks.

First, you must understand how property law works, what its goals are, and why everyone benefits from it. Property law (at least in the American system) is designed with one goal in mind: to move goods to their highest and best use. This goal is accomplished by encouraging people to own and develop items, land, or ideas and controlling those assets so they can be put to their highest and best use.

Highest and best use? What does that mean? It is the idea that a single object has more value to one person than to another. For example, a wedding ring means much more to the person for whom that ring symbolizes their enduring commitment to their spouse than it means to a metal scrapper.

It is important to distinguish the difference between the theoretical highest and best use that is the design of property law and the end result of the allocation of resources in a capitalist system. An object does not get to its highest and best use simply because someone is willing and able to spend more money on it than another person. For example, food thrown in the garbage by a wealthy American would reach a higher use if it was consumed by something that needed it for sustenance. Simply because the current system we have fails to move an object to that highest and best use does not change the goal of the system.

Ownership Creates an Incentive to Improve Things

"Property Law" is the system of rules that govern how we allocate ownership in our society. At the basest level, the idea that ownership can exist at all is a part of our system of property law. Ownership is a useful rule to abide by, because it creates an incentive to make objects better (in the eye of the beholder).

Imagine that I own a piece of wood in stick form that I picked up from a fallen tree branch. That object exists in that capacity regardless of any human intervention in its composition. Imagine further that I take that stick and carve it into a fire poker that can be used to roast hot dogs over a fire. Now that object has been changed by the application of my time and effort and intellect and, as a result, it is more suitable for the purpose for which it may be employed. If in my imaginary world someone can come along and simply take that stick from me, then what incentive do I have to make the stick more useful for my purposes than it would have been without my time and intellect and energy? In essence my effort is wasted, which rationally justifies my choice to never invest the effort in creating the hot dog roasting stick in the first place.

Carving a stick such that I can roast hot dogs with it is simple and easy. However, alter that example only slightly and instead of making a stick that can better roast hot dogs, I carve a beautiful intricate carving that takes me months of effort and skill to accomplish. It is easy to see that the underlying concept of the application of effort to objects for their betterment would certainly be disincentivized without the ability to own an object. To a degree it is owning an object, but it is important to remember that to a degree owning the object that has been improved by my effort, energy, and intellect simply means that I own the value produced by my exercise of time, effort, energy, and intellect—even if at the end of the day the result is an object that exists in the real world.

There is no immutable rule imposed on humanity that things may be owned. Indeed, if there is only one person on the planet then ownership doesn't really make much sense at all. (Why would I own a piece of land if there is no other human against whom that ownership can be enforced?) We want ownership because it justifies the application of human effort to the improvement of an object.

Property Laws (in America) Assign Ownership and Allow Control over Disposition of Property

When most people think of property they think of personal property or real property (land). Personal property is all sorts of objects that are not land. Things like the clothes you are wearing or a computer or a car are all types of personal property. But this category also includes other objects that you may not think of as personal property including a satellite in orbit. The common characteristics of personal property are that the objects are real and exist in the real world (i.e., tangible) and that they are movable (in the sense that they are not permanently fixed to one specific location the way land is).

Real property is land. It is different from personal property in that you cannot (from a human perspective) pick up a piece of land and move it. While, in theory, it is possible to move land by scooping it up with a shovel and moving it to a new spot, what you are really doing in that moment is changing the nature of the property from real property to personal property by removing it from the geographic space that is the land.

Our criminal justice system punishes those that violate property law. Because we have a system dedicated and equipped and authorized to enforce property laws via criminal law, I am substantially less motivated to spend my time and energy protecting my stuff, while still having an incentive to improve it. When I leave for work in the morning I am confident that if someone breaks into my house and takes my stuff that the police will respond to protect my interest in that stuff. This system of protection that exists and takes property law seriously allows me to have confidence that those who would otherwise violate the property law rules will be held to account and disincentivized from breaking into my house and taking my stuff because of the fear of the potential consequences.

For the majority of us, this basic criminal system offers sufficient protection of our personal and real property at little individual expense. The things in my house are very important to me and very much worth protecting in my opinion, but without sufficient economic value, I just couldn't justify the salary required to provide that actual protection through private security. Lucky for me, I live in a city that has a police department and a criminal justice system that spreads the cost and provides me with a layer of protection that gives me confidence that my property won't be taken or destroyed as soon as it leaves my line of sight.

But what about property that is not moveable or tangible—like ideas or designs? That is where intellectual property laws come in. Intellectual property laws were designed as part of the great ideas the American founding fathers put into our federal constitution. As such, they are protected under Article I, Section 8, Clause 8 of the United States Constitution and enforced by both civil and criminal sanctions. Criminal sanctions come from the Department of Justice and civil sanctions come in the form of a lawsuit either enjoining the unlawful activity or suing for damages for the violation of the intellectual property law right.

In American intellectual property law we have four types of intellectual property: (1) trademarks, (2) copyrights, (3) patents, and (4) trade secrets. Each type allocates ownership and protects property in a different way.

Trademark

A trademark is just what it sounds like—a trade mark. Stated another way it is a marking used in trade that can only be used by the holder of the trademark. The purpose of this area of intellectual property law is to provide consumers a means by which they can identify the thing they are attempting to acquire.

Imagine a world where all soda cans are without labels. You head into the grocery store and literally stare down an aisle of aluminum cans with no idea which can contains beer and which can contains juice. That world is very confusing. Even worse, imagine a world where anyone is allowed to use a Pepsi label on their can regardless of what is inside the can. I could sell cans of water with a Pepsi label and make a lot of money. So yeah, this area is pretty simple: our goal is just to allow the owner of the trademark exclusive use of the marking such that people can identify the item they are acquiring with certainty that the object will be what it purports to be.

The expiration of a trademark is when it ceases to provide its function as a trademark either because it has been abandoned by the holder (for example the company that owns the trademark ceases to operate for a period of time) or because it fails to identify a specific product anymore (for example trampoline, hovercraft and videotape have all become so generic that they fail to specify a product anymore such that they no longer function as a trademark).

Copyright

A copyright is a right to copy the work. Stated another way it is a unique presentation of an idea that is protected against exact reproduction. The purpose of this area of intellectual property law is to provide makers of unique works the ability to control the fruits of their labor. Why spend days working to get exactly the right angle on a photograph of a rare wild cat if, in the end, that photograph can be stolen and infinitely reproduced by any person who sees it? Without the protection over the exact copy of the work, we are unable to provide the maker of that work with a financial incentive sufficient to justify the expense of generating the work. If a person spends years writing a play called *Hamilton* but can't profit from that effort (and genius) after the work is created, then why would the maker invest so much time and energy and effort to develop the play? Simply stated, we provide artificial scarcity over the idea as a way to convince people to spend their time making better ideas.

Importantly, the expiration of a copyright is time. The end result of the copyright on the work is that it goes into the public domain. That's right: to gain copyright protection you must give up the long-term ability to control the idea. So, for the copyright holder it is a trade-off whereby the maker generates the work and can control it for a time, but then ultimately loses control of the idea so that the public gains the benefit of the work for all remaining time.

Patents

Patents are a time-limited license to control an idea that is novel and unobvious. These things are brilliant. Essentially, you just reduce an idea to usable form (it can't just be an idea, it has to be real). Then you get to control the disposition of that asset to the exclusion of all others. Once the time limit expires (fifteen years for many patents), then the idea is free for anyone to use and is publicly available for anyone who wants to find it. This allows a person to invest in the development of an idea and recuperate that investment if the idea is a good idea such that under the principles of property law (Step 1) the patent owner is able to extract a capital value from the sale of the idea as a result of the idea being worth more than the money spent to another person.

Like copyrights these are time-limited in their duration, and the end result is that the knowledge gets moved into the public domain and anyone can use it. A great example of how this is valuable is in terms of generic drugs. Companies developing treatments for diseases spend a lot of money on researching and developing those treatments so that they can monetize the results of that work. For example, think about the COVID-19 vaccine created by Pfizer; that is all that Pfizer does—it makes ideas in the form of treatments or vaccines or drugs and then sells them to the public. In order to gain that exclusive ability to develop and sell that idea, Pfizer must get a patent—and to get a patent, they must show the rest of the world (through the Patent and Trademark Office) how to make the thing they want to control. Once the time limit expires, that knowledge is free to anyone who wants to use it, and any business or person that wants to manufacture the drug at a cheaper price is able to do that from that point forward. Rather than charging a high price for the drug to recoup the investment into the invention of the drug, those companies try to manufacture the drug at the cheapest possible price and make it available generically.

Eventually, the generic drugs become available to people at a substantially lower price and—for the lowest price that some generic manufacturer is able to make the drug available—the public gains the benefit of being able to access an idea that Pfizer invested in inventing.

Trade Secrets

Trade secrets are secrets held within a business. Frankly, they are kind of stupid. They remain secret as long as they remain secrets, and the best example of a trade secret is either a customer list or the formula to Coca-Cola. Both of which have very little value outside of their trades, but quite a bit of value to the holder of the trade secret. The goal of this area of the law is to take away the incentive for rival companies to steal trade secrets from each other. If they do, they will be barred from using the secret anyway, so then why spend time trying to steal it? Truly boring stuff except in a very limited circumstance.

Using Intellectual Property Laws to Create Artificial Scarcity Gives Ideas Value in a Capitalist System

The main difference between intellectual property and real or personal property is the scarcity of the object. In order to be as clear as I can be, by scarcity I simply mean that the object itself is not infinitely reproducible. It may be true that there are multiple houses that exist, but only one of those houses is my house, and while I can replace my house or destroy it or get a new one, nothing changes the fact that my house currently exists in its current form in its current spot on the planet, and it is physically impossible to replicate it in the exact same spot such that I would have two identical houses that I could use. Stated another way, the house is scarce because it is not replicable. It is obvious by the nature of the object that a car is not infinitely reproducible at minimal cost. In fact, it takes quite a bit of effort and resources to create a car. If I started building one from scratch today (including designing it myself and mining the components), I doubt I would be able to finish the car before the end of my life.

To go full circle, ideas and other intangible concepts are not scarce because they can be easily reproduced at a negligible cost. For example, many people know that two plus two is four. That knowledge is easily replicable because it exists solely within a human mind and as a result it can be replicated in equal number to the number of human minds that exist. Further, that replication occurs at a very minimal cost because you need only explain to someone why two plus two equals four, and if they are capable of comprehending that, the idea then exists in their mind with the only cost being the time taken to explain that to the person.

Truly, intellectual property law is very simple, although it may appear complicated on its face. Recognizing that ideas are infinitely reproducible with little or no cost we must apply artificial scarcity to ideas in order to provide those ideas with value. Artificial scarcity is simply the idea that by law or other mechanism you create scarcity where none exists. A great example is downloading a copy of a song. While the song may actually exist on your computer in easily useable form, we apply law (in this case copyright law) to make that song artificially scarce—and, thus, of value in a capitalist system— even though it is not really scarce in the real world, so that we have the ability to use property law as a way to move those ideas to their highest and best use. Importantly, when you purchase a song for download you aren't actually purchasing the right to control the copyright of the song. You are purchasing a license to be able to listen to the song when you want, as often as you want.

The control over the property law right goes to the copyright owner, who is generally the maker of the copyrighted thing. Dave Chappelle complains about the theft of his ideas regularly now that he understands what was taken from him during his time working on *Chappelle's Show*. In a funny (or tragic) juxtaposition *Chappelle's Show* did not actually belong to Mr. Chappelle. He entered a deal with a company (Comedy Central, I think) that made money by developing ideas in the form of television programming. Apparently, Mr. Chappelle was paid in a lump sum to generate that television programming, which was ultimately owned by the company. In theory, the company took a risk in the first season by betting on the show's success by paying people to create the show, which gave Mr. Chapelle the economic justification to spend his time generating the ideas that are the show without going bankrupt. After it was clear that the show was a success, however, the risk was so substantially mitigated that it could reasonably be considered theft to pay Mr. Chappelle only a portion of the value he created in making the show. Further, by making that payment in the form of a one-time payment (a salary) instead of as residual profit on the value of the copyright for its existence (the life of Mr. Chappelle plus seventy years under current copyright law), it becomes clear that the copyright owner will generate substantially more economic value from the ideas of Dave Chappelle than Mr. Chappelle will gain from his own ideas. Thus, Mr. Chappelle feels (probably correctly) cheated out of the economic value of his effort and intellect.

So, to bring this back full circle to how, under copyright law, an idea is moved to its highest and best use, we must understand that this statement is made from the perspective of the copyright holder, not from the perspective of the licensee of the copyright or the consumer of the copyrighted thing. Currently, the copyright owner of *Chappelle's Show* believes that the highest and best use of the copyrighted work is to leverage the show economically by delivering it for free (or a small price) to any consumer and collecting revenue for allowing that use. The economic value of that use may be in the form of advertising dollars or in the form of payments for use in a streaming service. *Chappelle's Show* may be a good example of the system working less than perfectly, but the result for our purposes is the same: (1) *Chappelle's Show* gets created and (2) we, as consumers of the copyrighted work, get access to the results of that intellect and effort for an extremely low price (almost negligible). That the proceeds of the economic value of the idea are probably distributed unfairly doesn't change the series of incentives within which we can justify the creation of the show to begin with.

Intellectual Property Laws Have Successfully Incentivized Society to Generate Better Ideas

I know that intellectual property laws are effective at generating new ideas because with literally no effort we walk around this world and enjoy the benefits of the investment of other people in making ideas that we enjoy.

Intellectual property laws have allowed for massive leaps in what we can experience. I can turn on a radio (made by IP investment a long time ago, but very cheap in the modern world) and hear an awesome song that captivates me. It is beyond my capacity to generate a song as great as what I get for free from Taylor Swift. But for copyright protection she could not justify the investment necessary to generate those songs. I can walk through a Walmart and buy a toaster with super cool functions I would never have dreamed of. Made of materials I don't have the time to design. Manufactured in an efficient way such that it is presented to me at the lowest possible cost to produce the object. But for patent law, we wouldn't have the toaster, nor the materials, nor the manufacturing process because but for the ability to protect those things against theft, a person would not be able to justify their investment in the development of those ideas. I can open the app store (on my phone) and get a free app that shows me the other side of the world, a cool game, or any one of hundreds of millions of useful functions (and some very non-useful functions). What justified the investment into the development of those apps? That's right—intellectual property laws.

A cool aspect here that illustrates the value creation aspect of this is in relation to the cost of the TV in my bedroom. A few months ago, my wife and I decided we wanted a new flat screen TV in our bedroom so that we could relocate the current TV to the spare room for the benefit of my mother-in-law. We went to Walmart and got a fifty-five-inch flatscreen smart TV for $498. If I was to start building right now it would take me likely several thousand hours to build an object close to that TV (but it would probably be all janky). If I work at the federal minimum wage of $7.25, the value of the TV is roughly equal to sixty-nine hours of my labor. If I spent only sixty-nine hours trying to build that same TV, I wouldn't even get close to building it, and yet, I have the TV. When you look at it that way it is a pretty cool conglomeration of human effort that moves dirt into TVs and TVs into my bedroom. We will explore this concept further below.

In order to be clear that ideas exist far outside of technology, let's explore an example that has nothing to do with any technological advancement. According to US Patent 6,368,227B1 on November 17, 2000, a man named Steven Olson from St. Paul, Minnesota, applied for—and was eventually granted—a patent for "Method of swinging on a swing" described in the abstract as "A method of swing on a swing is disclosed, in which a user positioned on a standard swing suspended by two chains from a substantially horizontal tree branch induces side to side motion by pulling alternately on one chain and then the other." The swing was not new, but how to use that swing to generate a new effect was, apparently, a novel and unobvious way to swing on a swing. I seriously doubt that this patent was of any economic value to its inventor, but the end result remains that the person invested their time, energy, and effort into the generation of an idea (how to swing on a swing) and took the time, energy, and effort to write it down, draw some pictures, explain it to the US Patent and Trademark Office, pay the fee, and record for the benefit of anyone willing to look, his method for swinging on a swing. If I was to start from scratch and have no idea what to do with an object I encountered that happened to be a swing, I could search patents and find out at least one method for using a swing that is described in the patent.

Intellectual property law allows people to control things (ideas) that are otherwise uncontrollable. That control allows for the capitalization on the idea, which in turn creates the incentive to take that risk and generate the ideas in the first place. When coupled with property law, this allows ideas to get to their highest and best use.

Understand Intellectual Property Law

CHAPTER 4

Putting an Idea to Its Highest and Best Use (i.e., Getting Solutions to Where They Need to Go)

I OFTEN ASK NEW EMPLOYEES, "IF I SENT YOU INTO THE woods right now with nothing but a hatchet, how long before you come back with an iPhone?" Some people are clever and answer "It depends on how long it takes me to find a person with an iPhone and rob them." But the real answer is, "Never. I will die long before I am able to successfully build an iPhone." It is a truth of our world that is often overlooked. A single human on this planet by themselves would never learn how to find and mine the minerals necessary to make an iPhone. Then invent and mold plastic as well as a touchscreen. Then invent and manufacture the computer apparatus needed to power the phone. Then learn how to build an operating system and a programming language. Then learn how to program the phone to work. The amount of human effort and intellect required to create the object is simply so vast that it cannot reasonably be accomplished within a human lifetime. Yet, at the same time, most of us could walk into a store right now and acquire the object that we could never create in our lifetime.

I then follow up this lesson with why we have access to such a complex good at a level of effort far below what it would take to actually create the good if we were to do it ourselves. Say, for example, an iPhone costs $2,000, and I am a McDonald's worker making $15 an hour. In theory, it would take about 134 hours of labor working at McDonald's (so 3.35 weeks) to generate enough income to justify the purchase of an iPhone. Compare that to the millions of hours it would take for me to build that same iPhone by myself.

Why am I able to make such a trade?

The answer is obviously because of how our property law system orients incentives over a period of time to justify the application of human effort and intellect such that the iPhone can be made available to me at that lower labor value. In part, this highlights the value of working together cooperatively as a society, but more importantly it shows the insanely valuable tool that we have at our disposal to create stuff and then move it to where it is most valued.

Ownership and property law rules are designed by people from a human perspective to effectuate human goals. Property law (at least in the American system) is designed with one goal in mind: to move goods to their highest and best use. What does that mean? It is the idea that a single object has more value to one person than to another. Currently, we use property law as a system by which we can measure that value in a way that allows for ownership to change if the value to the current owner is less than what a ready buyer is willing to value the thing at. Let's expand further how a wedding ring gets to its highest and best use and whether it can ever stay there.

As a brief aside, we use money as the fluid to measure the relative value of the object among people. Using money as standard currency for the transaction, you can move the wedding ring to its highest and best use through a series of independent transactions. Imagine a world where a ring made of silver travels over the course of a few hundred years through human history.

Initially, the ring is nothing more than unrefined metal that exists on or in the ground somewhere. That metal is found and worth enough to the finder to justify taking that metal from its current resting place. Next, because the unrefined metal likely has less value to the finder than it does to the metal refiner, the metal gets sold to someone who has tools and equipment to make that unrefined metal into raw silver. Next, the raw silver is sold to a jeweler who values the metal more highly than the refiner because the jeweler can form the metal into a beautiful wedding ring. Next, after the ring is formed, the jeweler sells the ring to a young woman who thinks it is a wonderful object to give to her husband on their wedding day. Next, the ring is given to the husband who treasures the ring more than any other person on the planet (because of its emotional value to him), which is why the ring never gets sold by the man.

Until, one day, the marriage falls into disrepair when the husband finds out that the wife has been cheating on him and he must get a divorce. Now, that same ring is sold to a pawn shop owner who values the ring more highly than the husband. To the husband it has become a source of pain; to the pawn shop owner it is a source of revenue. The pawn shop owner then sells the ring to a young man who gives the ring to his husband. That couple has one child and remains married until their deaths. At which time, the ring is transferred to the child as a family heirloom; the child cherishes the ring as a memory of her parents until she decides to pass the ring on to her adult child. The adult child, who in this example has a serious drug problem and has never met his grandparents, then sells the ring to a drug dealer for the child's drug of choice.

The ring story could continue forever, on and on and on, as the ring gets transferred from one person who values the ring less highly to a person who values the ring more highly. This story also shows how even the same object (a chunk of silver) can be valuable to a person in one time and quantity, but not in another.

These examples demonstrate how and why property law moves goods to their highest and best use. This principle can, and is, applied to every object that exists. A tampon is likely worth more to a human with a vagina than a human without one, and that same tampon is likely more valuable to a person currently menstruating than to a currently non-menstruating person. A pair of size nine men's shoes is likely more valuable to a man who wears size nine shoes than to a woman who wears size twelve shoes; a Cowboys football jersey is likely more valuable to a person who likes the Cowboys than a person who likes the Dolphins. Similarly, the Cowboys football jersey is likely more valuable to a jersey collector than to a person who is not a football fan. Pepsi is likely more valuable to people who like Pepsi than to Coke drinkers. Cigarettes are likely more valuable to a smoker than to a nonsmoker. A motorcycle is likely more valuable to a motorcycle rider than a three year old. An Apple product is likely more valuable to an Apple fan than to a PC user.

On and on and on for every single object that exists. The object for one reason or another will always be more valuable to one person than another no matter what the object is (even nuclear waste is more valuable to a person who can refine nuclear waste than to a person who cannot put that nuclear waste to use).

How does this apply to intellectual property law you ask? Ideas, when given artificial scarcity, are also moved to their highest and best use by the forces of property law and capitalism. The rules of ownership enabled and protected by property laws allow the property owners to use the property to their highest advantage, depending on their needs or desires. For example, on March 21, 2023, the company Blackberry announced that it had entered into an agreement to sell its patents to an investment group called Key Patent Innovations for $900 million in cash and royalties. How in the world can a set of ideas be worth $900 million? Because the company purchasing those patents believes it can monetize those ideas for the remaining duration of the patent period such that it will generate more than $900 million in revenue, thereby justifying the purchase. Why would Blackberry sell the patents if they could just generate that revenue themselves from the idea? Because for whatever reason (which is truly immaterial) Blackberry doesn't want to put the ideas to use. It is very likely that the management for the Blackberry company has decided they do not want to continue on as a business and that they would rather wind things up than continue to try and force the public to like Blackberry as a brand. As you can see, the ability to monetize the idea through artificial scarcity and push it into the property law/capitalist system has created an incentive and a justification to direct human effort and energy and intellect toward the generation of a better idea.

The Relationship between Property Law and Capitalism

It is not correct to say that because the purpose of property law is to move goods to their highest and best use that the system always generates that result. As we've seen in the examples above, there are many factors that go into the determination that an object (or land) or idea or design or trademark is more valuable to one person than another. But even if getting an object to its highest and best use isn't always achieved, the purpose remains the same. If we keep in mind that getting an object to its highest and best use is the goal of property law, in general, and that capitalism supplies the human motive to accomplish that goal, and that humans are the means by which the goal is accomplished, we can understand the inevitable truth that there are always factors affecting our ability to accomplish that goal that are beyond our control. At that point, we can shift focus and stop being concerned with the system itself and instead move our focus to the errors within the system.

Capitalism and Its Effects on the Intellectual Property System

I will briefly explain my understanding of capitalism and how it relates to intellectual property law such that collectively the net effect is to direct human effort, energy, and intellect toward solving problems that need an idea as a solution.

According to ChatGPT:

Capitalism is an economic system that is based on private ownership of the means of production and the creation of goods and services for profit. In a capitalist system, individuals and businesses own and operate the resources used to produce goods and services, such as factories, land, and equipment.

Under capitalism, the market forces of supply and demand determine the prices of goods and services. This means that producers are motivated to create goods and services that people want to buy, in order to make a profit. Consumers, in turn, are free to choose the products and services they want to purchase, based on their own preferences and needs.

One of the key features of capitalism is competition. In a competitive market, businesses must strive to create better products and services at lower prices in order to attract customers and make a profit. This competition helps to drive innovation and efficiency, as businesses seek to gain a competitive advantage over their rivals.

Capitalism also encourages the accumulation of wealth, as individuals and businesses are free to keep the profits they earn from their endeavors. This can lead to income inequality, as some individuals and businesses are able to accumulate greater wealth than others.

Overall, capitalism has been a powerful force in driving economic growth and innovation, but it also has its drawbacks, such as income inequality and the potential for exploitation of workers and resources.

In my mind, capitalism is very good at aligning incentives such that humans are motivated toward the end result of increasing the overall quantity of goods and services available to all humans. Frankly, there isn't a better system that currently exists to accomplish that goal. Capitalism, however, is not good at all at allocating within a society the fruits of the greater quantity of goods and services available to all humans. Currently, it is nearly self-evident that there is a point at which so much wealth is concentrated under a single human that even with effort they would be unable to run out of wealth. While this may be advisable for people who generate that wealth themselves, it gets harder and harder to justify the further we get away from the human who generated the wealth. It is understandable that a motivation to generate wealth could be the ability to use it for the benefit of your spouse and children (I certainly am only motivated to a point to generate wealth for the benefit of myself; that motivation extends much further when the goal is to benefit the people I love after I am no longer able to care for them directly). It is certainly true that at a point it becomes extremely difficult to justify generational wealth that is removed by multiples from the individual who generated the wealth. I often wonder if this system is effective at motivating human behavior toward the end result of generating a higher quantity of goods and services. If it isn't, then we should probably reevaluate the system for efficacy purposes to determine if or how it can or should be revised.

Importantly, capitalism relies on predictions and generalizations of human desire and behavior in order to motivate the production of more (More of what? Stuff that can be owned). At our core, humans require stuff to exist. We require oxygen, water, temperature regulation, and food to even continue our own existence for even a short period of time. Our bodies tell us when we are thirsty, or cold, or hungry, or suffocating in order to motivate (if not compel) the result that we provide our bodies with what we need to survive. The motivation isn't even rational—it is below rational—it comes in response to how our bodies tell us to operate. Beyond the basic stuff that we must necessarily have to live, there are things that almost all of us desire to such a degree that they can properly be characterized as necessary for survival: things like love, family, someone to communicate with, the ability to be heard, the ability to move, satisfaction of curiosity, physical comfort, etc. If we can agree that humans will pursue love, if given the chance, and that humans are rational enough to understand how to pursue that love effectively, then we can draw conclusions from that such that we can predict what other stuff humans desire and will be motivated to produce. Best example: on her birthday I give my wife a nice card with a cool picture and a phrase I think she will enjoy. I don't do it because I think that paper arranged in a certain way with ink on it is somehow valuable; I do it because I am pretty sure that the time and energy and effort spent will show my wife that I care about her and her happiness, which makes her feel loved and likely causes her to feel more affection toward me. Thus, is the card worth eight dollars? Absolutely, if the thing I get in return is the opportunity to spend time feeling good about showing a person who I love that I care about them. Is the card worth eight dollars to my German Shepard? Nope, to her it is just a chew toy and probably worth less than a stick I can find in the backyard.

Capitalism and Property Law Are Not Perfect Systems but They Are the Most Effective Systems We Are Aware of When Accomplishing the Goal of Motivating the Creation of More Stuff

It is certainly true that this system has its flaws. But, as I said, it doesn't matter because as you will see we can fix it. Because the system we know to work best at generating, sorting, recording, and conveying ideas quickly is through the interaction of property law, IP law, and capitalism, it will become clear (assuming I am able to effectively communicate to you) that using that same system will also provide us with the ideas that we need to fix the flaws within the system best able to generate ideas.

One of the greatest examples of the problems that can result from our system of property law is the example of a person with an illness that will cause their death imminently. If the ill person happens to be a billionaire and one singular dose of the cure is currently owned by a homeless person, the homeless person could likely get several hundred million dollars for the cure, even if it only cost the homeless person a few dollars to make the cure. The combined impact of the need for the good to sustain the life of the billionaire and the scarcity of goods available to effectuate the goal of continued survival creates this problem.

To connect the dots: if capitalism is an economic system that, via ownership, and on the assumption of a human desire to increase their own wellbeing and the wellbeing of those they care about, creates the net effect that humans are more likely to spend their time doing things that generate the amount of return that the human desires, then we can passively direct human effort toward things others are willing to pay for (i.e., deem valuable). Property law is the backbone of that system because without ownership there is no incentive to acquire. Intellectual property law as a subset of property law creates the ability to own an idea and thereby, an incentive to create the idea to begin with.

Hopefully you can see that, as a consequence of how and why humans are motivated to do things, that systems applying incentives can direct that application of effort and intellect toward a particular end. Using capitalism as an example, if the system is really good at increasing the overall amount of stuff that is created by humans, but not very good at distributing that stuff among the humans such that overall human capacity is maximized, then we can recognize that as a potential problem. Because we are unable to immediately point to an obvious and agreed solution that will effectively solve that problem, we can then determine that we need a better idea to solve this issue. After making that determination, we simply use intellectual property law as the economic incentive (controlling the idea on the back end justifies investing the time and energy and expense to create the idea on the front end) to motivate human behavior to study the problem, theorize solutions, test solutions, and then spit out an idea that has greater efficacy. All of the stars align to effectuate that goal if it is possible to patent a system of rules that were designed to produce greater overall human capacity and could provably accomplish that goal. The obviously better system by which we accomplish that goal of idea generation (as we have seen occur over at least the last hundred years) is to have Disney invest in creating a movie rather than having professors at a film school create a movie. Is it possible that the film professors stumble upon a better system? Yes. But is one of those two entities obviously better and consistently better at generating a better idea (in this case a movie) because they can justify a substantially higher investment into the generation of that idea? I think the answer is obviously yes. The same system can (and should) be used to solve any of the inefficiencies that arise in capitalism.

Protecting and Incentivizing Ideas Is How We Generate the Best Solutions

THE APPLICATION OF INTELLECTUAL PROPERTY LAW TO any problem that needs an idea as a solution is clearly the best system humans have generated thus far to create better ideas and solve problems. To be sure I am being clear, when I say, "Problems that need an idea as the solution," I am saying problems for which we don't already have an obvious solution. For example, a human with a broken leg may have died as a result of that broken leg throughout most of human history. Today, for the most part, we have solved that issue and a broken leg is not a death sentence. If I were to break my leg right now, I don't need an idea to solve that problem, what I need is to go to the hospital and allow medical staff to use the solutions they already have to fix the problem. I am not sure if that is clear, but I am doing my best. I will give you another example just to be safe. I do not need an idea to solve the problem of how I keep my feet from getting cut by the harsh ground of the earth upon which I walk. I don't need an idea because that problem was solved long ago. I don't need an idea; I need shoes.

Using Patent Law to Generate Public Policy Solutions

Because the type of ideas that we need to solve these public policy problems are valuable in terms of their function, it is the function of the idea that needs to be protected (as opposed to a copyright that protects the arrangement of the idea rather than the function). Because we need to protect the function of the idea in order to justify the investment into the creation of an idea that functions better than our current ideas, the most natural fit would be patent law systems.

Currently the US Patent and Trademark Office (USPTO) classifies patents into three subtypes: (a) utility, (b) design, and (c) plant. Let's dive a little deeper into these categories to describe the alternate solution that either utility patents be available for these types of problems, or in the alternative, that a new category of patent be devised for the purpose of promoting useful functions in the public policy sphere.

According to the USPTO website, "Utility patents may be granted to anyone who invents or discovers any new and useful process, machine, article of manufacture, or compositions of matters, or any new useful improvement thereof." Stated simply, the patent protects the idea in terms of its usefulness. This is the system where we theoretically will gain the most ground in the public policy sphere because the thing to be protected is the process by which you create a reduction in drunk driving incidents, or the process by which you create a reduction in the number of homeless people living on the streets, etc. The use, the utility, the process is the part of the idea to be protected—not necessarily its particular form, but rather the function of the idea.

According to the USPTO website, "Design patents may be granted to anyone who invents a new, original, and ornamental design for an article of manufacture." The best recent example is the dispute between Apple and Samsung relating to infringement of Apple's design patent for an iPhone and in particular the "black rectangular front face with rounded corners and its grid of sixteen colorful icons on a black screen." It may seem simple to us now, after Apple invested into the design of an iPhone, that of course you would want rounded corners so that the user doesn't get poked by square corners, or that sixteen app icons arranged against a black backdrop is a good organizational format for app icons on a device that size. But to realize why Apple gets a time-limited license for creating that design is the key. All of us benefit from their investment into that design and in time, because their patent is publicly available and describes the design, anyone can design a phone the same way because Apple learned how to do it and taught the rest of us. In fairness, Samsung could have arranged the app icons in a single row, or a circle, or with only two icons on the screen, or in the same way that Microsoft arranged apps on its phone. It seems less user friendly than the iPhone design, and in time, everyone will be able to copy the iPhone design for free.

According to the USPTO website, "Plant patents may be granted to anyone who invents or discovers and asexually reproduces any distinct and new variety of plant." This type of patent is pretty specific, right? But to Monsanto and their multiple billion dollar company, this is exactly the way that they are able to justify inventing in the agricultural space and making new and possibly better genetically engineered plants. Reasonable people can disagree about whether this type of patent is useful. Personally, I find it irrelevant to the problem we are trying to solve within this book.

Alright, now that we have seen the three types I hope you can see why using utility patents or design patents would be ideal approaches to solving public policy problems. The government could enable the use of utility patents for public policy systems (like a criminal justice system, how to organize a Department of Motor Vehicles, or how to implement policies that more efficiently address the issue with people living on the streets). Using design patents for these problems is a little more complicated. In essence, you would be trying to build a new patent type that allows for ownership over novel and unobvious solutions to public policy problems in a way that protects the utility of that idea for a period of time in exchange for teaching the rest of the world how to solve the problem.

For example, a new system could, in theory, allow for a time-limited license (say fifteen years) over a public policy solution that has a likelihood of reducing instances of drunk driving deaths that can be monetized by apportioning the cost reduction in the real world of that idea in part to the patent holder (inventor) and in part to the government that chooses to purchase that patent. In that system, the ideas that will rise to the top will be those ideas that actually create a cost reduction that a government led by democratically elected leaders can choose to purchase or not. The incentive from the perspective of the idea generator is that they will try to target areas that will make them the most money (i.e., achieve the greatest cost reduction to the government that may purchase the idea) such that when deciding what ideas to invest in, the generator will target those areas where they perceive (and hope) they will be able to provide the greatest benefit to the government and to all of us who exist (and future generations), because we are now investing in ideas that will solve the public policy problems we face now and in the future, and we are doing it in a way that deliberately directs human effort and intellect toward that goal in a pragmatically effective way. Ta-da!! Your society will passively get better through the end result of the machinations of the incentives to direct human effort and energy for that purpose as a result of how capitalism directs those efforts. Yay!!

However, when there are no such protections in place, like patents protected by intellectual property law, people cannot justify their investment—their time, energy, research, and resources—to solve a problem. Consequently, that problem will remain unsolved.

The best example of how and why we need to apply intellectual property law protection to every problem that needs an idea to solve it is the juxtaposition of the growth of the medical field and the legal field over the past 150 years. Just look around and you will obviously see that our ability to fix medical problems has vastly improved in 150 years. Why? Because of patents on medical products and procedures. But because no such intellectual property law protection exists such that lawyers can effectively patent and monetize their systemic revisions, we are left in a world where our legal system is virtually stagnant compared to the medical field.

There are a multitude of other problems that could be solved if we had an incentive and legal protection for coming up with solutions.

Want a better criminal justice system? Develop a system of intellectual property law that allows makers of that system to justify the time and money spent generating that better system. *But, can't I get a patent for a criminal justice system?* Yes, but you cannot enforce it against a state (your largest customer by a long shot) because they are immune from suit in federal court unless they waive that immunity. Do you think any state has waived immunity from patent lawsuits regarding criminal justice systems? Not at the time I wrote this (4/17/2021).

Want a more efficient and effective way to petition your government for redress? Me too! But unfortunately no one has invested to generate that idea, and as a result, the system doesn't exist.

I could spend a million dollars and a year developing the best criminal justice system in the world. But what would I do with it? Even if every state agreed that my system was vastly better, they would just steal the idea from me and I couldn't justify the initial investment. Thus, I don't make that investment. Like you, I don't want to go bankrupt developing an idea that I have virtually zero possibility of ever being able to control. I have bills like everyone else, and as much as I would like to do the work, I cannot justify it because my family and employees count on me to continue generating income instead of fixing the problems that could be fixed with an investment into generating that better system.

Financial Rewards Incentivize Some People to Generate Better Ideas Sometimes

Because we exist in capitalism (here in America), as much as we may want to spend our time and energy generating better ideas, most of us are unable to survive in this world unless we are able to gain financial rewards for our effort. Some people are motivated by financial reward, and if they are motivated by financial gain, then that system is sufficient; but even if they are not, it is impossible to invest in the generation of the better idea without the ability to get the financial reward because of the limitations on the structure of capitalism.

One of the oddities of our current world is how companies can justify the investment of literally hundreds of millions of dollars into the generation of algorithmic stock trading programs. The only thing these computer programs do is attempt to make money by executing trades very quickly on the stock market. I cannot in any real sense explain how this is a good thing for our society, but unsurprisingly the money gets invested for this purpose whether I like it or not, because the net effect of the incentives of our world is such that by spending the money and time and effort generating the computer program, the person can justify the investment by its expected (and now demonstrated) ability to generate more revenue than it cost to develop the program. Because the incentives are designed as they are, we reach the inevitable conclusion that we will always reach, which is that time and energy and money will be invested in the generation of ideas that have the capacity to generate more money than was invested to create them. Obviously not every investment into the generation of an idea actually results in an idea that generates more money than was invested in it. That is the risk that some of us take in order to have a chance to make the future better. And when it does work out, it is beneficial that all of us now have the idea that didn't previously exist.

From a personal perspective, I am not currently motivated to invest in ideas that generate more money for myself. I am not personally motivated by the desire to gain money for the sake of gaining money. I live cheaply and will live a very happy life with very little money. I am motivated to help people, and because I understand that I was born into capitalism, I know that the greatest mechanism by which I am able to help people is through the mechanism of capitalism such that I can use that system to empower people to make each other's lives better. From a government's/society/public perspective, though, arguably the government is motivated to save money. However, I really don't think the government cares about saving money at all (which is part of the problem). The idea here is that in order to convince a government to make the choice that it is more efficient and effective for our society, we will have to provide evidence that the solution is so superior that to choose not to employ it is obviously the wrong choice. Thus, if I can come up with an idea that saves the government money, and I can use intellectual property laws to patent and then license my idea to the government, we both win and a social problem can be solved.

For example, while I was writing this book I began working on developing a criminal justice system for reducing drunk driving deaths. From my perspective, this is low-hanging fruit in the sense that it is a problem that has been studied and tracked already relatively extensively. At the end of the analysis we discovered that the insurance industry considered the cost of a drunk driving death to be north of four million dollars on average. NHTSA (the National Highway Traffic Safety Administration) considered the estimated loss higher at over eleven million dollars per death. ODOT (the Oregon Department of Transportation) had the figure somewhere above nine million. As a result of these numbers we are able to accurately conclude that if we can save one life by avoiding one drunk driving death, it would be worth spending at least four million dollars to accomplish that goal.[2] Or you could think of it in terms of it saving our society/government/the

---

2   I understand the reductionist and frankly heartless nature of turning something as emotional as a drunk driving death into something as emotionless as a dollar figure. But I recognized the necessity and value of this approach when someone pushed back against the proposed program by saying, "Well gosh what would that cost our government to enact." If the pricing structure is juxtaposed against the proposed cost savings then the fact that it costs a lot doesn't matter because the result is a greater cost savings. Further, there is this cool and not to be forgotten side benefit that we saved a life. The even cooler part that most people would never even consider is that we actually saved two lives, the drunk driver who doesn't spend years in prison and the rest of their life feeling terrible because they killed someone, and the human who didn't die.

taxpayers four million dollars; and as a side note we happen to also be saving the life of a fellow human (I hope you can feel the tone of that side note).

The cost analysis is different for the insurance industry and ODOT and NHTSA. But an example of the types of things that we will save money on include: (1) the raw economic value of the person who didn't die through their ability to generate economic activity, (2) the cost for the police to respond to a crash, (3) the cost for medical personnel to respond to the crash, (4) the cost to incarcerate the drunk driver, (5) the cost to the trial court system to process the case, (6) the use of prosecuting attorney resources to prosecute the person, (7) the use of criminal defense resources to defend the person, (8) the property damage costs for the crashed vehicle or vehicles, (9) the lost economic potential of the drunk driving offender, (10) the cost to supervise the offender after release from incarceration, and (11) the cost to the appellate court system in dealing with any issues that result from the incident, etc.

The true loss when the event occurs has a sprawling impact on our collective resources. All of those costs are human effort that need not be employed and could be expended in a different and more beneficial way if we could just stop the drunk driving crash from ever occurring.

We took a look at who the offenders were that were causing these drunk driving deaths and found that a substantial portion of these offenders were not on their first drunk driving offense. However, during their previous offenses, we failed to employ our sentencing mechanisms effectively such that we were able to effectuate a reduction in that particular drunk driving death. The data appeared to show that we could get a reduction in recidivism for several years of roughly 30 percent to over 50 percent on repeat offenders by simply using some of the characteristics of the programs we know to work to our benefit.

To provide an example, in 2011 NHTSA published a report entitled "An Evaluation of Intensive Supervision Programs for Serious DWI Offenders" and in it they concluded:

> The reductions in recidivism ranged from 54.1% in Oregon up to 8 years post-offense, to 30.6% in Minnesota up to 4 years post-offense, to 18.1% in New York up to 5 years post-offense. The evidence appears to be strong that ISPs (Intensive Supervision Programs) with the following common features can be very effective:
>
> - Screening and assessment of offenders for the extent of their alcohol/substance abuse problem
> - Relatively long-term, close monitoring and supervision of the offenders, especially for alcohol and other drug use or abuse
> - Encouragement by officials to successfully complete the program requirements
> - The threat of jail for noncompliance

In 2019, there were 167 drunk driving deaths within the state of Oregon. Assume the lowest value of preventing the drunk driving crash to be four million dollars. Assume the lowest possible reduction in recidivism of 18.1 percent up to five years after the program. With those assumptions, these systems, if employed, could in theory, create a reduction in drunk driving deaths by about thirty people over the course of a year within the state of Oregon alone. This would save society upward of 120 million dollars each year.

So, if I had the money, time, energy, and ability to patent a novel and unobvious system that taught people how to reduce the instances of a drunk driving crash death via punishment through a court system, I could market the idea to courts and they could pay a fee to incorporate it into their sentencing systems. I would profit from the licensing fees and the state would save millions of dollars each year. Frankly, it does not matter what the licensing fee is within this system. The greater the licensing fee the greater the projected profit from creating the property right to control the idea, which means more can be invested on the front end to create the idea. If the licensing fee percentage is less, then the projected profits are lower and less money can justifiably be risked in support of generating the idea that is the solution to the problem currently facing our society. Stated another way, if you have a low licensing fee, you can justify a smaller investment; if you have a high licensing fee, you can justify a greater investment. To be clear, the amount of the fee doesn't matter; either choice will have consequences, and as the system is implemented, it can be adjusted to create an incentive to produce a different result.

One of the key features by which I would price out these public policy solutions would be to simply take a portion of the cost saved by the entity that enacts the policy. As above, I think the proper alignment of incentives is to allow those ideas that create the most efficient system and are endorsed by the elected leaders to be those ideas that rise to the top. By creating a pricing structure that is directly linked to the result achieved (in terms of cost-savings), you have a theoretical alignment of incentives between the government and an idea producer that will cause the idea producer to approach the generation of the solution to the problem in terms of cost-savings for results achieved (i.e., efficiency).

The beauty of protecting ideas using intellectual property laws is that it isn't the end of the road. Imagine if intellectual property law concepts were applied to redesign intellectual property law (boom! Meta). We would abandon using the rock we currently use to try and screw something in and start using a screwdriver. We would then generate a better screwdriver, and one day someone will make a drill. When that happens the world will begin producing better ideas and solving more problems at such a quick pace that the issues we are currently trying to solve will be laughably easy to solve by our descendants. We owe it to them to try.

As I've explained, we must first find a way to create the financial incentive to generate the data needed to understand the problems and apply mental energy to determine how we solve these problems. If we don't, then the problems will remain, and we are blindly failing to use the best tool we have available to solve problems in our society. Unless/until we get on board with this approach of incentivizing solutions through intellectual property principles, we are destined as a society to sort of flounder around and hope that we stumble upon improvements to the world's problems. I say we use the tool we have to solve the problem.

Apply Intellectual Property Law to Any Problem That Needs an Idea as a Solution (Notably in the Public Policy Realm)

CHAPTER 6

The Application of Intellectual Property Principles to Real-Life Problems

HOW DO WE FIX HOMELESSNESS? HOW DO WE IMPROVE the criminal justice system? How do we stop a rioter from wanting to riot? Or a country from wanting to engage in a war? Or two gangs from starting or continuing a turf war? I don't know—no one does. People think that they know, but they really have no idea. However, as I was writing this book, I was also in the process of trying to show that the idea of applying intellectual property law principles to public policy problems can and will work. As one starting point, we began to look at chronic homelessness as one place where we could possibly apply intellectual property laws successfully to solve a problem. We didn't know what we would find, but what we found was insight much deeper and more useful than we ever expected.

Solving the Problem of Homelessness

Let's pause for a moment and determine whether we need an idea to solve this problem or if, rather than an idea, we need something else. My math on this question is simply: do we already know how to solve this problem or do reasonable people disagree about what the problem is and how best to approach it? Chronic homelessness is an easy place to render the determination that we need an idea to solve this problem. I know this to be true because you will get different answers from smart people about how to fix chronic homelessness. Some people will convincingly tell you that the solution is simply more treatment for drug addiction, that the people on the streets are largely drug addicts and need help solving that problem, and then the housing part will solve itself. Some people will tell you that homelessness is the natural result of rent being "too damn high!" and that if we could just get rent control in place these people could afford a place to live and would move back off the street. Some people will tell you that the street people are just mentally ill people and that the homelessness problem only started when we closed the mental hospitals, and if we just opened more mental hospitals the problem would be fixed. Some people will simply tell you to screw the homeless—either they pull themselves up by their bootstraps or they die in the streets, or maybe the purge is a good idea. Some people will tell you that homeless people just don't want to work, they would rather panhandle, and if we make panhandling illegal, they will be forced to get jobs and stop leeching off of society. The truth is that none of those explanations are correct in all circumstances, but rather, the truth is that we simply do not understand the problem with great enough precision to even begin solving it.

I want to juxtapose this series of explanations (all of which may be correct, or they all may be totally wrong) with a group of doctors trying to fix your broken leg. Imagine one doctor saying that the broken leg is beyond repair, and we must simply cut it off to save the body (i.e., purge the homeless), and another says we need to apply a blood clotting agent to stop the bleeding, and then the leg will heal itself (i.e., address the most immediate symptom of the problem and give the problem time to resolve itself; stated another way, more drug addiction treatment or mental health support or rent reduction), and yet another who says the real problem is thin bones, and we just need to get you more calcium to make the bones stronger so that they don't break anymore (i.e., make panhandling illegal). It is obvious to us in the modern world that none of those solutions are correct and those doctors have no idea what they are talking about or how the human body works. But the only reason we have the knowledge necessary to understand the problem and solve it is because many humans over a long period of time worked deliberately to understand and solve the problem of a broken leg.

So, as you can see, because of how people discuss and argue about the problem of chronic homelessness, it is obvious that we as humans don't yet understand why these people are chronically homeless, and unless we get extremely lucky and guess the right answer, we are hopeless to fix it unless we have a better idea. Below we will discuss how to approach the problem such that you can generate the knowledge necessary to understand the problem sufficiently to begin testing hypotheses that may or may not solve the problem.

Here is my approach to trying to prove that intellectual property law will, in fact, provide the correct incentives to solve these problems in the form of my attempt to show that problems can be solved by the application of intellectual property law principles. I wanted to show this by (1) better understanding chronic homelessness such that we could see what, if anything, could be done to fix chronic homelessness and (2) rethinking the goals of the criminal justice system to see if there is a better way to achieve them. Of course, right now, there is no other incentive for me to do this, except that I am interested in making the world better. However, I undertook these investigations and have imagined how I could use the information if I were able to, say, patent my ideas. I chose to look at these two particular problems because frankly the problems look very solvable to me, but for some reason my society fails to solve them.

The first step in applying the approach I've been suggesting is identifying whether there is a problem that requires an idea as a solution.

Obviously, getting to the root of the problem is not always easy. If you would like to read the full details of the process Hunking Law, LLC Special Projects used to gain a deeper understanding of homelessness, please refer to the appendix.

When it came to investigating homelessness, the category we saw as the biggest problem for society is what we classified as "chronic" homelessness. These folks have been living on the streets for over six months and are what I would consider to be the classic conception of a homeless person. These people are the ones causing the economic harm to society through occupying police resources, fire department resources, ambulance resources, cleanup resources, responses from mental health professionals, etc.

Does "chronic" homelessness require an idea as a solution? Yes, because no one yet knows how to solve the problem. If they did, it would be inarguable in the general scope of the solution.

Next, we identified the most cost-effective ways we could help alleviate the problem because the best way to create an idea that will be adopted by a government is to design it such that it is so superior an idea that to not adopt it would be silly. What our research then revealed was that the most cost-effective way to remove the chronically homeless from the streets would be to meet them where they are at mentally, physically, and emotionally, and person by person begin identifying and providing tools to help the person fix the problems that are causing them to be on the streets.

We discovered that the primary path by which chronically homeless people get to that position is getting kicked out of public housing for one reason or another. Even though there can be good reasons why people get kicked out of public housing (e.g., building a meth lab in your apartment) we must still be able to realize the unobvious that the effect of kicking them out is likely that we are creating a homeless person.

This helped us understand that the most cost-effective way to keep people from becoming chronically homeless is to ensure they have a place to live prior to getting evicted from public housing.

So, the idea that we came up with, based on this information, is to add a precondition to eviction for government housing providers that requires the evictor to ensure the evictee has a place to live (that isn't the streets) prior to a court granting an eviction. The point at which we would begin the process of seeking patent protection for this idea is once it is reduced to usable form, but not more than 365 days after the idea has been prior art for itself. In essence, we would just seek protection for the idea once it becomes eligible for protection, but not after it loses its ability to be protected due to the fact that we did not seek said protection.

If our understanding is correct, implementing this idea should reduce the number of people becoming chronically homeless and help stop the flow of people onto the streets.

Next, we began evaluating what the appropriate number of resources were to spend on this problem. In order to justify purchasing this system we would need to convince a potential purchaser (The government. Which government? Pick one.) that by buying this system it would clearly benefit them (i.e., that they are getting a good deal). In essence, because the government is currently allocating a number of dollars toward this problem, if you total up what they are currently spending and can show a projected reduction in homelessness of, say, 5 percent, then the value of the idea to the government is total cost paid currently to solve this problem less that same number reduced by 5 percent minus one unit. That means that I can project a positive return on investment if I spend not more than the final number in the calculation above. If I know that number, I can make a plan to invest to solve the problem and then go out and find people who want to invest money into the solution of that problem, and they have at least some likelihood of not losing all their money, but instead gaining a return on investment such that the trade was profitable and those profits can be reinvested into the next idea.

Since we don't have the actual numbers yet, I will plug in some fake numbers. Assume we have the following cost factors to consider: (a) cost of cleanup of campsites; (b) police/government response to clear campsites; (c) cost of police response to crime in a homeless camp to include the court costs, prosecution costs, and jail costs of incarcerating the person; (d) cost of fire department response to reckless burning (people need to stay warm by design); (e) cost of ambulance response for medical conditions induced by living in a harsh environment; (f) cost to businesses spent clearing unwanted campsites from their business (in the form of reduced taxable revenue); (g) cost of lost property tax revenue because taxpayers leave the area residentially and commercially; (h) cost of decreased property value such that assessed property tax is lower; (i) cost of lost economic activity that could result if the homeless person were able to be rehabilitated such that they could be gainfully employed; etc. (there are more variables, but for the purposes of this example we need not be perfectly comprehensive). Assume in each case the cost to the government is $10,000 (actual numbers are substantially higher, especially in large cities).

Ten categories (including etc.) means the government is currently paying $10,000 in a given time unit to deal with the problem of chronic homelessness. If a system is designed that provides a projected 5 percent reduction in cost to the government, the likely sales value of that system to the government is somewhere between $1 and $4,999. I like the thought of the idea generator sharing cost savings with the beneficiary of the better system (the government), so my proposal yields the result that the development of the system is worth $2,499.50 at maximum, and I can afford to invest at most $2,499.49 into the generation of the idea if my purpose is to generate profit to be reinvested in the next idea.

Let's use some fake numbers to express the relationship described above. Let's assume that a city (let's call it Atlanta since it begins with an A) currently spends one million dollars a year in costs associated with responding to the chronically homeless. I can say with virtual certainty that cost is vastly below the actual cost. Further, let's assume the idea is built and the system is tested and currently being implemented. Let's assume the cost of enacting the system (paying the people who run it) costs eight hundred thousand dollars a year. Thus, we have an actual cost savings of two hundred thousand dollars. Under my general conception the end result is that Atlanta saves one hundred thousand dollars and pays one hundred thousand dollars to the provider of the patented or otherwise controlled idea. Because the creator of the controlled idea is a business that intends to generate profit, that business then reinvests that money into the generation of the next idea that creates the cost savings. Thus, the system benefits everyone and helps us move our society forward faster. We have the ability to build better ideas for our world that will allow us to make our world better (whatever that means; for me, it means more efficient).

If we are able to find a fixed cost that will be produced by the expected cost reduction then we have a number against which we can measure anticipated cost reduction. The proper licensing fee for the idea (in my mind) is 50 percent of the actual cost reduction to the government entity licensing the program. In the real world, my proposal would be to package the idea up into a very pretty and cross-referenced presentation that includes slides, video, and a salesperson pitching to a government entity why this idea is worth their money.

As you can see, if intellectual property laws protected my idea, there would be a potential financial reward for me, and therefore, I would have greater incentive to research and develop my idea. But more importantly, people like me would be able to spend their time generating better ideas in the public policy realm because they would not need to do it as a charitable endeavor and could, instead, do it as a job. I, like everyone else, do not want to go bankrupt trying to fix the criminal justice system. Because currently I would go bankrupt trying to fix the system, I cannot justify spending my time, energy, and effort toward the accomplishment of that goal. If, instead, I could monetize the time spent working on fixing the problem, then I actually have the ability to fix things.

Fixing Our Criminal Justice System

Along with my research on homelessness, I have been trying to come up with ways to improve our criminal justice system. The criminal justice system isn't designed to try and fix social problems. It spends its time resolving conflicts one by one and assuming that the work being done is valuable to society based on after-the-fact rationalizations for why the system should be punishing people.

I am reminded of the purposes of punishment provided to me in criminal law class in law school.[3] At the time I didn't realize how silly it was to approach the world that way: (a) punish people for doing bad things (b) justify why we punish people. Basically, our current approach is not based on any evidence that indicates that punishments actually work: the purpose of punishment in today's criminal justice system is simply to punish the offender. Stated another way, we start with the presupposition that we must punish people for doing stuff we don't like (like spanking a child) and from that, recognizing that punishment is harmful by design, work backward to try and justify why we inflicted that harm. What's worse is that, in general, when the punishment doesn't work then we escalate the punishment (spank the child harder because, obviously, that would work, right?)

It can be said (and should be said) that to impose a punishment for the sake of punishment is cruel. Further, if we

---

3   According to Joshua Dressler (the guy who wrote the criminal law textbook used in my criminal law class in law school), the purposes of punishment are: (1) general deterrence (the idea that if we know something bad will happen if we rob a bank, we are less likely to choose to rob a bank), (2) specific deterrence (the idea that if we punish a bank robber for robbing a bank, that specific person will be less likely to rob a bank in the future), (3) incapacitation (the idea that since we can't figure out why a serial killer is killing people—a psychiatrist's problem—and because the harm a serial killer will inflict is extreme, we must then put the serial killer in a cage because any other choice allows a very serious harm to befall society), and (4) reformation (the idea that if we help make the bank robber a better person, they will be less likely to rob another bank).

have no reason to believe that the punishment imposed will improve the person or the conflict or the community, then how can we say it is anything other than cruel? Further still, even if we believe that the punishment we impose has some social benefit, and we can rationalize the punishment through the previously designated purposes of punishment, if we have no evidence to justify that supposition, then upon what basis are we able to pull this punishment out of the realm of cruel?

It is truly amazing that, unlike other professions and industries, the criminal justice system never thinks to take a step back to see if we can create a rational reason for doing what we do and develop the evidence to get in line with the rest of the world in trying to make evidence-based decisions that will effectuate justifiable goals. This is exactly what I am proposing and am currently working on trying to figure out how to do. I want to at least begin generating that evidence which can be analyzed over a period of time to solve the twin justifiable goals of a justice system: (1) reduce instances of future undesirable behavior[4] and (2) resolve the feeling of injustice that accrues in a victim of a crime. In order to accomplish that goal, the approach would be to understand why the behavior occurred, study responses to that behavior, and determine which responses (i.e., punishment) create a greater likelihood that the behavior will not occur in the future. The ability to monetize this system flows from the hope that by reducing instances of undesirable behavior via incentives that operate passively, it will cost less than to

---

4   You may be wondering why we would limit ourselves to simply reducing FUTURE instances of undesirable behavior as opposed to remedying instances of past undesirable behavior. This may sound a little silly, but it is because we don't have a time machine. Frankly, we cannot control the past instances of undesirable behavior. We can't bring the murder victim back to life or stop the drunk driver from crashing. We just don't have the capacity to affect the past. We can, however, at least try to affect the future. If we don't try, then nothing will ever get better.

actively respond to instances of undesirable behavior. Side note: we will also, in theory, be able to lessen the likelihood that the bad behavior happens at all.

Protecting Ideas Justifies Investing Resources to Develop Them

Being able to protect my ideas to solve the problems of homelessness and criminal justice and exert ownership over them justifies the time, energy, and resources that I have invested into them. The hope of financial reward for myself and society at large makes me want to come up with more ideas. If I continue to generate more ideas and then invest my efforts, and others do the same, we will be that much closer to fixing our world.

This same process can be used to generate all sorts of good ideas that will solve the problems we face together. I think the coolest part of this is that the idea itself can be used to generate an even better idea for how to generate better ideas. We can accelerate how we find solutions to problems in our world. Any cost savings thereby generated will help make our overall system more efficient. Further still, we will be allowing all those good ideas that people have to make the world better to be tested and vetted and turned into real solutions. Stated another way, we can tap into the collective creative value of all humans and provide them with the means and the method by which they can apply that human creativity for the benefit of all of us.

CHAPTER 7 {.dingbat}

Implementing This Approach on a Global Level

SO, IF YOU ARE STILL WITH ME AT THIS POINT, YOU MAY be wondering how we best approach building the apparatus that organizes the effort and intellect such that the investment into the generation of better ideas can be realized. Frankly, this is where I don't have the answers. I have a suspicion that I will need to prove the concept myself by building an organization that can make this theory into a reality. However, I am not a corporation builder. There are others who are much better at that task than I would ever care to be. So, let's just walk through. We should approach this problem in the same way that we approach the criminal justice system and homelessness. (1) Identify the problem that needs a solution. (2) Determine whether we need an idea or something else to solve the problem. (3) If we need an idea to solve a problem, begin by trying to understand the problem better through research. (4) Theorize as to which systemic revisions are likely to best solve the problem based on the results of the research. (5) Test the theories and identify evidence that identifies what works and to what degree it works. (6) Because we have hopefully just generated a novel and unobvious idea reduced to usable form, go get a patent on the idea. (7) Sell the solution to any entity that wants to purchase the idea. (8) Identify another problem and use the proceeds of the first patent to fund the solution to the next problem. (9) Just keep doing this until you run out of problems to solve (which is likely never).

Creating an Organization to Create Better Ideas

Idea number one is to simply build a corporation that will operate like Pfizer does to create better ideas in the realm of public policy. The advantage of this is that a corporation is a known quantity. As a result of our experience with medical companies creating new ideas using this approach, we do know that it will, in fact, likely be an effective mechanism by which we create those better ideas. However, there are some notable concerns with this approach. In particular, the profit motive can be easily abused to the detriment of normal people; for example, Martin Shkreli purchased the intellectual property rights to a drug and famously raised the price extraordinarily high even though it was a life-saving treatment for some people. That issue is ever-present as the conflict inherent in the desire to promote the profit motive has the potential to cause a truly bad (albeit temporary) scenario for some.

You may ask how this is different from a think tank. The difference is the funding source, which creates a different incentive. Disney makes money by risking its capital toward the generation of an idea in the hopes it will generate profit. Disney does not take charitable contributions or government grants and use that money to make movies. As a result, the movies generated by Disney are regularly a heck of a lot better than the movies created by charity. Furthermore, a substantially larger amount of human effort can be directed toward the creation of a Disney movie because Disney knows how much money it can expect to make on an idea and, as a result, knows how much money it is worth to generate the movie. Even further, Disney can (and does) purchase insurance on the movies it creates so that it can mitigate the risk that a movie will be a financial flop and that they will lose a lot of money. The interactions of these incentives are simply not possible within the construct of a think tank because a think tank has different needs in order to continue its own survival. Its survival does not depend on whether it, as an organization, is able to generate an idea that will successfully make society more efficient. Its survival depends on its ability to keep the people who provide the funding to create the think tank happy.

Idea number two would be to keep the company as a privately owned company. Cargill is an example of a company that is privately owned but also able to innovate and get things done. The downside of this model, in my mind, is the reliance on the good of individuals in order to create the better ideas. Ultimately I think that this model is easily corruptible and not substantially better than using a corporation.

Idea number three is frankly the best I have currently. To my mind, the problem of ownership for the mechanism that invests in innovation is the concentrated benefit that could very easily be misused. This issue, coupled with the subject matter of the innovation, could very easily be turned into something that is not used for a proper purpose. For example, if the rich and the powerful want to design public policy systems that benefit themselves and those like them, it could be done pretty quickly and without a control on the improper exercise of the tool. Because the ideas themselves are for the benefit of everyone (presumably public policy should benefit everyone [exception (there always is one) is that serial killers probably don't personally benefit from a system of criminal justice that imprisons them for life]), the mechanism should be owned by everyone. To me that is the best (and maybe the only) way by which you can properly incentivize the non-corruption of the mechanism. I just don't see any other way. Sure, this system could also be bad in that it may destroy itself (by the owners choosing not to reinvest, but rather take their money now in the form of dividends); it will certainly favor solving problems that are being felt as problems by a larger group of people (this isn't a bug, it is a feature) and it may be that people outside the organization seek to influence it by improper means. However, it appears to me that those problems are solvable by the system itself, and I would hope that the mechanism can solve those problems without someone directing it toward that end but rather as the cumulative effect of the net effect of the will of all the owners.

So how does idea three work in the real world? It would be tough logistically, but essentially you have a corporation that is owned by every person in equal, nontransferable shares. Each share dissolves upon the death of the holder and new shares are created when a new human is born. Each share has a single vote (this part would be extremely difficult to coordinate but, like all problems, it is solvable), and people, like shareholders, will be able to vote their shares as they please. There is likely a better model for this system, but I personally don't know what it is. As a result, this is the best I have, people.

If anyone has a better idea, please let me know.

Selling the Idea to Those Who Have the Power to Implement It

Importantly, in order to actually see this (or any) system actually get derived and implemented, it must be sold to the people with the power to implement it. Let me pause for a moment and explain how I view selling something. I view it in two components. Component A is as it seems, literally selling something to a person for money. It involves setting a price, communicating the price to the other side and what they will get for that price, and then actually having money (or any other measure of value) change hands to get paid. Component B is really more selling in the sense of persuasion. Like when a car salesman chats you up on the car lot and tries to make the buying experience more fluid and friendly and to persuade you toward a certain vehicle. Both of those sub-components are included in my conception of selling. Back to the original point, in order to turn any of these systems into reality, they will need to be sold to the people who have the ability to implement them.

This naturally invites the next question, *what is the best way to sell the ideas?* In my mind, the only way to really get any of this sold (by which I mean getting society to agree that this way of generating ideas will be faster and more effective) is to show that the new system is so vastly superior to the old system that to not buy it would be silly. In order for us to adopt self-driving cars, it is not enough that the cars be as safe as people, but rather they must be vastly safer than human drivers. In order for us to switch from the horse and buggy to the automobile, the automobile must be so superior to the horse and buggy that to use a horse and buggy would be silly. The only alternative (because humans are slow to adapt) is to slowly allow us to die off and for new generations to adopt the idea because they are more comfortable with it. However, that approach is much, much slower than simply proving that the idea is so superior that to not adopt it would be silly.

The System May Be Slow and Scary to Change but That Shouldn't Stop Us from Trying to Change It

It is easy to see why people are frustrated when dealing with systems that fail to improve very quickly. Because of the above principles, it should now also be obvious why those problems are failing to get fixed. Simply stated, the reason those problems are getting fixed slowly is because the system by which we are attempting to solve the problems doesn't do a very good job of trying to fix them.

That said, some of the pushback on changing systems is natural. Humans have a natural fear of the unknown and adjusting a system substantially and quickly causes a natural trepidation in every person (including me) who looks at the system. However, if we want things to improve, we have to take a risk in trying to change them (except that to just jump headfirst without any evidence or hope that the change will be valuable is about as stupid as using our current system to try and make better ideas; in fact, changing a system without evidence that it will be better is exactly as stupid and slow as using our current system).

One particular experience of mine is illustrative here. In 2011, I was working for a legislator while I was in law school. I was pulled over by a police officer and asked to provide auto-insurance proof. I couldn't find it within the vehicle, but I did, in fact, have car insurance. Naturally, the police officer wrote me a ticket for failure to carry proof of insurance.

When I went to court (because I am a smart-ass and was in law school) I hand-created an insurance card by literally tracing the printed insurance card. When I gave it to the judge, he came absolutely unglued, but he gave the hand-written proof of insurance to court staff and had them call the insurance company to verify insurance coverage was in effect when I was driving, and then dismissed my ticket. So, I went back to my job at the legislature and called the DMV legislative policy analyst and asked if the DMV would entertain a change in the law to not require written proof of insurance, but rather to allow electronic proof of insurance to be sufficient. I got a lot of pushback from the DMV on this; they sort of looked into it and then abandoned it. It wasn't until years later that the law was changed to allow people to use electronic proof of insurance.

Just saying, things adapt slowly and to sell these ideas in the real world, there will need to be substantial improvements to the current system.

CHAPTER 8

Working Together to Create a Better World

WHEN ELON MUSK SET OUT TO MAKE LOW EARTH ORBIT more accessible, he didn't decide that the best way to do it was on his own in his backyard on the weekends. Nor did he determine the best way to make electric cars more accessible all alone. He used the tools that we have to best effectuate a goal: he used intellectual property law systems and hired people in order to direct them and expend organized effort toward the accomplishment of the goal. That is how we actually get things done.

Ultimately, if we want a better world, we are going to need ideas to make it better. I think the progress of the intellectual property law system has far exceeded anything the founding fathers ever dreamed of. Stated more simply, the intellectual property law system worked, and it worked a lot better than they could even conceptualize at the time.

In the realm of patents, I don't believe any of the American founding fathers could have ever dreamed that we would have spaceships that could put humans on the moon, or cell phones that could instantly connect people across the planet, or solar electricity-generating devices that could power a Tesla. In the realm of copyrights, I don't believe any of the American founding fathers could have ever dreamed that a

Marvel movie would exist using CGI technology to create a moving picture that looks real, or that dubstep could exist as a series of sounds.

Instead, the intellectual property system allowed for ideas to be layered on top of each other throughout hundreds of years, and the result is that we are able to enjoy the fruits of all that effort and intellect without individually investing it.

As I have shown, applying intellectual property laws to public policy problems is only one example of how we can organize human effort and intellect in the most effective and efficient way. But it is the best idea I have right now. Creating a system for ownership and incentivizing improvements to one's intellectual property justifies a person's (or society's) investment in that property. When a system is in place to protect those investments, people feel free to keep creating and generating more ideas. We can then use the resulting data to see which ideas are the best and most cost-effective for solving the problems we are trying to solve. Just like our health system was able to develop COVID-19 vaccines in record time, we would see huge leaps in how quickly we could address problems that have plagued us for centuries.

On my desk, I have a note to remind myself of one of my weaknesses as a person. The note says simply "Ask for Help." Generally, my normal way of operating in this world is such that asking for help is not how I tend to solve problems. However, I am smart enough to recognize how dumb I really am and that other humans are much easier or better or faster at solving problems that I cannot. To mitigate against falling prey to my own weaknesses I have a constant reminder to quite simply ask for help. In solving a problem as large as how to best solve problems in our society, I think it is necessary that I ask for help. Thus, I am asking.

So to be sure we close this loop—I believe I have explained, to the best of my ability, in the preceding chapters the three-step process to fix the world: (1) understand property law (including how capitalism intersects with this system), (2) understand intellectual property law, and (3) apply intellectual property law to any problem that needs an idea as a solution (but more specifically for my purposes to public policy problems).

If you think my idea about using intellectual property laws is a good one please spread the word or find another way to help us move toward a better system for solving problems. If you think I am wrong, please write me and let me know that you think I am wrong and why. If you don't know why, then just say it—sometimes a gut feeling is right even if it is currently inarticulable. If nothing else, I'm pretty confident that we both want the world to be better, and it is not going to change unless we at least start having conversations about it.

Analysis and Identification of the Problems within the Homeless Community

FIRST, I BEGAN BY SEEING IF RAW DATA WAS ALREADY available for us to review. Upon learning that very little recent or reliable information existed such that we would be able to understand who is chronically homeless and why, we began gathering the information ourselves. I hired an employee and sent him around the city to various places to begin to ask people who were homeless about who they were and what they thought caused their homelessness. We then took that information through the interview process and built it into a database to try and gather some hard information.

Once we gathered the hard information (about 110–120 interviews), we began categorizing the information so that we could see if there were any obvious trend lines that we should be paying attention to. There were two trend lines we found, which will be discussed at greater length below, and we used those trend lines to formulate two hypotheses. As of this writing, we are attempting to continue data gathering, expand information sources to verify the accuracy of the information we have, continue to build the database we have, and find a way to test the hypotheses. Certainly prior to the publishing of this book, and long before you are reading this, we should be further in the process of developing a protectible piece of intellectual property that will effectively reduce the overall collective economic cost of dealing with the homeless population.

The first trend line we noticed was based on our original goal of trying to understand who was chronically homeless and what was motivating them to be chronically homeless and determine if it could be fixed. Based on self-reporting, we found four sizable categories that collectively constituted the vast majority of the chronically homeless population. Those categories in descending order were: (1) active drug addiction, (2) mental illness, (3) domestic violence, and (4) fleeing abusive parents.

We found this trend line in our attempt to measure the problem (i.e., Why the heck do we have all these homeless people on the streets? Who are they, and why are they there?). This concept came as a result of listening to *The Armstrong and Getty Show* and agreeing with their perspective that if we don't know why all these people are out there, we can argue all day long about how we fix it and truly have no idea what we are talking about. To circle back to a previous example, we are medical professionals in the 1820s arguing about whether prayer, leeches, or a rain dance is more likely to cure cancer. Obviously, that argument is worthless and truly just reflects that we have no idea what the problem is and, thus, very little hope of knowing how to effectively address it.

We were originally looking to confirm or deny the popular conceptions for why we have so many homeless people. We looked at what I considered to be the major arguments: (1) They are lazy and don't want to work. (2) They are mentally ill. (3) They are drug addicts. (4) Rent is too damn high. First, to be clear about the subset of data we included in making our determination, we classified the level of homelessness the person was experiencing based on duration.

The first category was "transitory" homelessness. Most people have experienced this type of homelessness at one point or another. It is characterized by a very brief lack of housing defined by a lack of owned property sufficient to house a person or an effective rental agreement. I personally have been transitorily homeless multiple times in my life even though I don't consider myself to have been a homeless person. One example that immediately came to mind was when I came back from my deployment in Iraq. The Army was providing me housing while I was on active military orders, so I had absolutely no need to have a rental agreement in effect. For a few weeks after returning from deployment, I no longer had the military providing my place to live and hadn't yet found a new place to live. In this time period, I was actively looking for a place to live, had the funds to pay for it, and a desire to have a place to live. So even though I lived in a bedroom at my aunt's house for a few weeks while I secured an apartment, I was technically, though not in my mind, homeless. This happened again as I transitioned into my first home, but it hadn't closed yet. And again when I got divorced. And again when I transitioned from undergrad to law school. So, in my mind, this is not the type of person who is truly causing a drain on society and thus was not included in the subset of people we were trying to figure out how to get off the streets. Frankly, I really wasn't "on the streets" or otherwise a problem for society.

The "intermediate" category includes people who are without housing for more than one month, but less than six months. An example of someone in this category would be a mother and her children running from an abusive relationship and truly without resources to quickly secure new housing. Another example would be someone living in their car after losing their job and running out of money before finding a new job. These people are at risk of becoming chronically homeless, but what we found was that they have the easiest access to voluntary help from others within our society—specifically from religious organizations and family or friends, as well as established government-funded women's shelters. These people (though admittedly causing some economic detriment to society) are not really the massive problem that people see and think about when they are discussing how to fix homelessness.

The category we actually looked at as the biggest problem for society is what we classified as "chronic" homelessness. These folks have been living on the streets for over six months and are, what I would consider to be, the classic conception of a homeless person. These people are the ones causing the economic harm to society by occupying police resources, fire department resources, ambulance resources, cleanup resources, responses from mental health professionals, etc. As a result, this narrower category became the category we actually tried to address more thoroughly.

With these categories in mind, we took a look at those popular conceptions of how we fix homelessness as discussed above. Within this subcategory of people, we found absolutely no evidence that they were on the streets because the rent was too high. Frankly, even if rent was virtually free, many of these people would still live on the streets because rent prices have nothing to do with why they live on the streets. Further, there was very little evidence (a very, very small number of people by self-reporting, like one or two people) that the people who were chronically homeless were capable of working but choosing not to. Simply stated, many of these people are not unwilling to work, but rather are very unlikely to be employed either due to an ongoing issue (active drug addiction or mental illness), or due to incompetence such that they are not employable.

Initially when looking at the large categories of self-reported reasons for chronic homelessness, we took domestic violence, running from abusive parents, and mental illness and stuck them in a subcategory of things that are really outside of the control of the individual. Drug addiction we initially considered as within the control of the individual. However, this changed over time because the self-reporting generally reflected that a substantial majority of these people did not want to be drug addicts, but rather had hit the point of hopelessness such that they weren't even really trying anymore to control their addiction. At that point we shifted and, on balance, considered this category to also be beyond the control of the individual.

Once we determined that 80-plus percent of the motivation for chronic homelessness was beyond the control of the individual and due to some (from their perspective nearly insurmountable) immediate problem that was hampering their ability to be competent enough to get a place to live, we then created our hypothesis that the most cost-effective way to remove the chronically homeless from the streets would be to meet them where they were at mentally, physically, and emotionally and person by person begin identifying and providing tools to help the person fix the problems that were causing them to be on the streets.

The second trend line that became obvious was what I would call the funnel for how these people got to the streets. I had personally never thought about it before; in my mind there are levels of housing security that exist as follows in descending order of security: (1) housing by ownership, (2) housing by rent, (3) housing by others (friends, family, the military), and (4) public housing. We found by self-reporting that these chronically homeless people were not reaching the streets because they lost their home due to foreclosure, or that they were evicted by a place where they paid rent, nor by getting kicked out by friends or family or the military (though this was a large number of people in the temporarily homeless category). But rather, the funnel that gets these people to the streets is the eviction from, or loss of, public housing. There are some very legitimate reasons for people to get evicted from public housing (e.g., the person tried to burn the building down, the person was extremely loud and disruptive, the person was committing crimes against other public housing occupants, etc.), but what seems to be unrealized is that once a person is evicted from public housing, they are out of options and at least somewhat likely to end up as a chronically homeless person.

This second trend line led to the second hypothesis. That second hypothesis is that the most cost-effective way to keep people from becoming chronically homeless is to ensure they have a place to live prior to getting evicted from public housing.

Collectively the first and second hypothesis (if proven true) should (a) reduce the number of people becoming chronically homeless and (b) get those people who are currently chronically homeless off of the streets and into housing.

Next, we began evaluating what the appropriate number of resources were to spend on this problem. Although not complete at the time of this writing, we are beginning to gather effective cost data that includes all the economic loss associated with a chronically homeless person that is directly attributable to a city government. Once we know more completely what that number is we will need to develop an initial plan, which will, in theory, fix the problem and test it to determine efficacy over time. If we are able to find a fixed cost that will be produced by the expected cost reduction, then we have a number against which we can measure anticipated cost reduction. The proper licensing fee for the idea (in my mind) would be 50 percent of the actual cost reduction to the government entity licensing the program.